The Best Indian Poetry anthology series is the property of RLFPA Editions (OPC) Pvt Ltd—an imprint of RædLeaf Foundation for Poetry & Allied Arts (since 2012), not-for-profit, independent literary organization committed to promoting poetry and allied arts in India and abroad.

First Publication Date: Dec 10, 2018
ISBN: 978-81-939295-0-6
₹475 | US $15 | £12
Originally Published in Paperback
Cover Art: Shutterstock

Manufactured in India, published & funded
by RLFPA Editions (OPC) Pvt Ltd.

RLFPA EDITIONS
RLPOETRY.ORG

The BEST INDIAN POETRY 2018

Linda Ashok

Editor

CONTENTS

INTRODUCTION

Why amidst so many anthologies did I start with the *Best Indian Poetry* series? When I say anthologies, some of the best that come to my mind include *The Oxford India Anthology of Twelve Modern Indian Poets, The Penguin Book of Indian Poetry, 60 Indian Poets*, and *The Harper Collins Book of English Poetry*. And yet, this new enterprise of the *Best Indian Poetry*; what is it trying to achieve? Well, it took me from several months to a year's time to decide if I am sure of this intellectual and financial investment, most importantly my time, and probably the risk of launching something new as the canons continue to rule. But this is what I believe and I would hope you'll come to believe in due course of time that this entire pursuit is only a goodwill initiative for the poets of my country and diaspora—an organized activity that keeps me in the know of poetry as it evolves in its private space.

Would you know what actually contributes to the maturity of the English language? For me, this language offers cultures to inseminate it and breaks walls to welcome linguistic immigration. Capitalizing on these aspects, poetry in English is enjoying all the attention, and deservingly so. But, what has also happened here is that when an Asian poet, particularly from the subcontinent, submits to a journal in the West, the editor is not able to fully appreciate that "new" English the way they can appreciate "the English" spoken by their own kin. I am ready to believe that the editor has no ill-intention but I also speculate how an editor is expected to appreciate what they aren't familiar with; how can editors of the world relate to a poet from India talking about an imagery in which they recall the cow dung washed mud walls without meaning poverty or soliciting pity of the foreign magazine's editor?

Some of the distinct objectives that BIP endeavours to fulfill include, i) help foreign readers of poetry break ice with poetry from India, ii) support literary journals for their hard work toward shaping world literature, and iii) appreciate poets of Indian nationality (Anglophone & regional) who not only enrich Indian literature but contribute substantially to the diversity of world literature. Modelled after the eponymous *Best American Poetry* (BAP) series by the legendary David Lehman and his celebrity poetry editors since 1988, the *Best Indian Poetry* (BIP) series is, in simple words, a consolidated feature of poets with their works published in literary journals the previous year. The arrangement is logically funded by the fact that the literary journals will have almost a year's time to attract traffic (or more politely, readers) to appreciate their curation before they nominate their best to BIP.

46 Anglophone poets—isn't that exciting? The very first thing I would possibly do is to cancel my day's plans, occupy the quietest floor of the city library and start with an ask; "How many of them do I know?" Of course, I will only take a limited bite for the day and then unleash my curiosity, aided by the internet, to find out more about the poet until satisfied enough to move to the next. Well, this is certainly not directing your course of time with this anthology. You must have your own ways to enjoy it the way you want.

Back to the business of discussing why these poets matter and why they should be read, and how each one is contributing to world literature. There are poets in this compilation who are very young in their practice and those practicing the art for ages. Poetry by young practitioners reveals the meteoric influence of the internet on Anglophone poetry thereby rendering it both intellectual and aesthetic finesse. Because K. Satchidanandan rightly says that "history abandoned is a future lost," the works by senior poets in the country

serve for the historicity of contemporary developments in Indian poetics.
Poetry curated in this volume ranges from being strictly form-centric to form-bending. Poets of the country are cognizant of poetry happening elsewhere and particularly the young ones through their work prove to be very inclusive and embracing. I will certainly reserve commenting on the works any further to ensure this representation does not become too patronizing because voices here are sure and independent. Basically, you as a reader (or more like a poet) already know of what's happening in your immediate circle. It would be only liberating to seek change and welcome new ways of listening and seeing the world as *Best Indian Poetry* is vetted by my reading of poetry appreciated from Far East to wild, Wild West. Sure, we must meet for a dinner sometime and I'll explain what Salmon means to us and how we do it other than simply baking it with lime and pepper.

Too early to map by trend but of course that would be an interesting fodder for discourse for someone to figure what these poems from 2017 have in common. This holds true for poetry in translation too but the representation has been severely jilted by the fact that regional poets are not submit-to-a-literary-journal kind. I am confident that the 2019 issue will fulfill this as regional poets in India take notice of this new avenue which facilitates an intellectual engagement of their voices by the purveyors of poetry in world languages

The *Best Indian Poetry* or call it BIP is a comprehensive solution not only for editors, but for literary scholars, and students of poetry. BIP as an annual record of "the best" by Indian Anglophone poets and poets writing in 27 different Indian languages is a much-recommended study resource for students who might not be able to technically afford a visit to this vast country and yet would love to go all the way indulging in the foreign as an act of expanding one's poetic scholarship.

I do acknowledge BIP as an annual responsibility wherein if not dragged into the armpit of poetic philosophy debating what constitutes good poetry and deserving of representation, I'll be overwhelmed unearthing new voices. I am sure that with every edition, some poet or their poem will not make it to the list and that'll be disappointment misinterpreted as elitism of the series. Or worse, some poet in a matter of exclusion may just decide to retract completely in their pursuit of writing (I am aware of what rejection does to innocent and inexperienced aspirations). But I am sure of my intention and BIP is astute in its mission. It can be assured that BIP will never take sides of poets but poetry that rings of the fierce artistry of Indian literature interplayed with postmodern literary tropes of world poetics. And all these from my personal lens until I move on to recruiting guest editors in the years to come.

So, who said poetry cannot make anything happen? It does make a human happen to their surrounding and the *Best Indian Poetry* is here to bring the tectonic plates of the west and the east closer than ever, therefore, heralding a borderless celebration of poetry across colours, languages, and cultural quirks.

And yes, I thank Stephen Byrne for editorial assistance and all the participating literary journals for contributing to this discourse!

Linda Ashok
November 2018
Mumbai, India

ABBAS BAGASRAWALA

The first time Abbas wrote a half-decent poem, he got kissed by a girl (okay, okay not a girl but a young-ish English teacher with life scarring lipstick) in the writing class he was in, while in school. Since being kissed by girls was hailed as an extremely good thing in no uncertain terms in the all-boys school he was in, he delves in poetry as much as possible to have a repeat of the same. Trouble is, he's never again written a half-decent poem although he might argue that it is not for lack of trying.

ABBAS BAGASRAWALA

HOW TO ENTER A POEM

You can enter it like it is a mosque
where you leave your shoes outside,
carry with you a minor fear that they will probably be stolen
by the time you're done

Now head inwards into the stomach of the building
And perform the wuzu, the ritual act of cleansing:
        the precursor to all worship
        the precursor to all poetry

After this, find a corner,
    keep your face hidden
and wait for the poem to reveal itself to you
Let the religiosity of the moment wash over
you
like some great flood
        meant to teach you a lesson

Hope that no one catches you
when the poem comes, and you
        inappropriately snicker
like a change of spelling that may not bode well with true
believers

Prostrate yourself every now and then,
see if there are pieces of the poem on the ground
somewhere that may have gotten away from you

Wonder if more women in the place could help
the coming of the poem?
Wonder if more menstruating women in the place enrage the poem
out its hiding places—
the smell of   blood   injustice

Have the domes in the mosques

always been this perky? Will they, at some point,
droop with age,
too many men, and their ministrations?

Seek out your favourite Namaazi,
The man with the burnt face, and see him
                                                seek meter
  and rhyme
to a limerick about hell and heaven, pure and impure

Thank your luck that your poem when it will reveal
itself, will not be about the fear of some unseen
God, but will rather, provide wonder and solace,
a feeling of being loved finally—You are the creator,
this mosque was built to venerate.

ABHA IYENGER

At a Caferati meet in Khan Market in 2007, Abha performed a poem titled "I Am Not that Kind of Girl' for the first time and it was met with delighted applause. To date, those who have heard her recite the poem or have read it in Yearnings, like to pull her leg, calling her 'not that kind of girl'. It is wonderful when people associate one with a poem and remember it. There is another poem titled, 'Strange Lands' which was also extremely popular with her readers because they could connect with the idea of strangers sharing grief and love.

For more: abhaiyengar.com

ABHA IYENGER

YOU CANNOT TIE ME

You cannot tie me
to any one religion, to any one relationship,
to any one post, don't put a noose around my
neck Have you ever tried to tie the winds?
If you did, you would realize how frustrated it made you
I am nothing but wind; I shake the leaves,
I smooth hair and shift the sands,
here and there. I don't have any fixed abode, and it is
also uncertain when I may disappear
from your life. Experience my touch,
accept me the way I am. I am not a goat,
you will not be able to tie me to a post, my throat
you will not be able to cut, you cannot sacrifice me.
No, I am woman, accept me in this form alone,
A whiff of air that arrived to add beauty to your
life for a while. Only this is true, nothing else.

Originally published in Hindi. Translated by Author.

ABUL KALAM AZAD

Crushed in the Tokyo metro, rubbing his brown shoulders with tired strangers, he thought of the land he fled. A land that lynches his kind on the streets, that strips him naked and hooks him to the flagpole. He looked around for a home to spill his lonely heart, a roof to hide his exiled eyes, a flesh to warm his frozen kiss...When suddenly, as a dozing Japanese man gently drops onto his body, a thought sneaks into his bones, maybe the land he was looking for was in his heart, in all the words he sculpts there within its walls, maybe the roof he misses was stretched, all along, into his verses... maybe the only home Abul had, and will have, was poetry.

ABUL KALAM AZAD

SALARYMAN

Tall buildings
like ladders of raindrops
cursed by the sky
to never leave the earth

Trapped in that raindrop
he sits before a pale desk
dressed in freshly ironed
and crisply tucked-in clothes

a light gray shirt with no visible folds,
black trousers with a soft blue interior

A cloud with hidden memories
of the world that left him behind

toes dress their solitary wounds
with sweat inside polished shoes

Unheeding of the clock
that never stops ticking,
he works and works

A routine ,so deeply stitched,
that can't loosen the threads
without tearing the cloth

Night leaps into streets outside
almost unnoticed, like a distant
relative whose entry none awaits

Overworked bodies tumble in groups
out of brightly lit cubicles
inside rooms cleaned with conditions

Swiping cards of various hues, he
boards a train with red insides
holding onto a metal hanger with both his palms

Huddled chunks of dozing humans, so
close that one can smell the dreams
frozen in the other's eyes

He wiggles out
with lot of effort
a new book of poems
he bought with the money he saves

Verses with warm fingers
hold his drooping lids
in a spiral shaped like a sonnet

Moon waits patiently
for ways to slip through
the walls of enclosed trains

A voice nailed to the ceiling
announces the arrival of the destination,
the end of a silenced path

He gets out,
his eyes still drenched
in the syllables of a poem
yet to finish

A poem on love

elusive as the breeze
that haunts every storm

As he finishes it,
he gazes into the void before

He knows he missed his station
and the last train back

A man sitting by the shore of rainy tracks
with an umbrella spread out before, full
of cracks,
hums,

'Salaryman, Salaryman,
did you miss your station again?'

AMARENDRA PANDEY

Amrendra thinks that poetry creates the places where mysteries and enigmas of this well-defined world unfold; they sail, walk, saunter, turn into a gale, and sometimes cast a silence. In the summer of his third or fourth year of Ph.D., Amrendra discovered these secret lanes and streets. Poems, he imagines, are internal monologues beneath the physical presence of thoughts, voices, cries, calls of inanimate and living things.

AMARENDRA PANDEY

DARK CORNERS

This is the beginning of the 7th century. The night when I felt
a draught coming from the mountains. And in it, the pages
of an ancient anthology are fluttering and hovering in the
moonlight.
At the end of an empire, I watch a desert fox digging a hole
and the wind howls. The silvery mirage of silence dancing
and rambling at the far flat end.

This is the six decades of repetitions and riddles. The hexagon.
A library containing books in unknown language sinks slowly in
the marsh. But its white reflection on the lake-water grows larger
and larger in time.

And in it grows another world. Or many worlds. With the whirls,
with many shapes of clouds, with boomerangs which are thrown
again and again into the sky.

Where I walk in the evening March wind, I walk in the
September nights when the moon comes up, rises above the
window glasses
of this colony. Dogs sit near grocery stores. Peddlers and
shopkeepers barter food and tea with unknown travelers. Shout
names which drift and vanish in the squares, roads, balconies.
Ladies dress for the
dance, sweet sound of rustling stays among the boughs, and a
man crosses the road for attending the cinema. Or many men
and women did.

It feels incredible that it happened. Any of it. The appearance of
scenes one after another. Every person is coming from the past,
and yet appears simple without

contradictions -

Like the presence of nothingness, obvious and unverifiable.

Like the time when I was going to the office in the placidity of trees and sky, and I was left with an image of myself as a boy, who is standing still on the ground, who is surrounded by other boys and above him a swarm of dragonflies.
They are saying to this child - you will remember us one day, you will remember this wetness of the wind, this whiteness of sky through our wings.

AMRENDRA PANDEY

AT THE OBSERVATORY

It is the place where, without admixture or confusion, all the places of the world, seen from every angle, coexist. — *J L Borges, The Aleph*

From this height everything seems clear
as if everything starting afresh.
Everything encased in one glance. Trees all hushed after the rain.
The birds.
The soft blue mountains.

Bog people are sleeping beneath these layers.
An arm-ring in the evening light, a decayed rope, a metal coin,
all ringing in a strange silent space,
except their bodies which are merged in the mire.

At the horizon the smoke rises, a somnolent sound fills the valley.
I hear an ancient tune – partly recognizable, partly unfamiliar.
Then the mild glow of the observatory, its domes, make me present.
And I realize a man is always divided – into the past and future, up and beneath.

And at the same time, everything continues to coexist, still always at a certain distance, not so near that you can grasp, not so far that you can ignore.

Near this sea, once the village of Tollund man would have felt the green glow on their skins, reflection of the universe on the clear beach.
Now a city, a lighted visage, is showing the sounds of the screeching planes,

clinking of the rusted metal trains,
melodious voices of the empty elevators.
Thousands of breathing bodies are walking briskly.
And at a distance not very far these places are vanishing while spiraling an invisible center.

In the midst, which is in itself an end,
I see the rushing wind on my face, one arm of our galaxy, and in its dim light my cold legs leaving a long trail inside this black ancient water.

AMIT SHANKAR SAHA

One fine day waking up from a beautiful dream Amit Shankar Saha found that he has managed to fly by those nets while the gods were paring their fingernails. Someone had once told him to stay unsettled, to stay alive. So he resigned to his fate of getting burnt in trying to catch the stars. There he found a room of his own and named it *Balconies of Time*. His incredible journey is archived in his blog Amit's Diary. He is now in search of the fugitive who writes his poems.

For more: amitss6.blogspot.in

AMIT SHANKAR SAHA

DELILAH

Delilah,
why don't you now
cut my locks of memories too?

In the dark they all come back,
every bit...
dense as the night.

When all the lights go to sleep
we grow our cropped hair
once again long.

The dust of your days
settles on my eyes
layers on layers.

But in your starved mind
philistine thoughts betray
all thoughts of us.

Good that my eyes are gouged out
for don't we all today
gaze eyeless at Gaza.

AMIT SHANKAR SAHA

RAIN INSIDE

It is raining inside me
But you can't see,
Clouds of words enter me
But you can't see.

It always rains in Macondo,
Do you know?
A hundred years of solitude inside me,
Do you know?

You come back from a holiday in Venice,
Too exhausted to enjoy the rains;
I stay quarantined in Oran,
Too exhausted to enjoy the rains.

The precipitation inside me
Dissolves my soul,
Distills my tears,
Dilates my heart,
Dilutes my orgasm;
You know, you see,
But you are too exhausted
Of all the rains, outside me.

ANNIE ZAIDI

Annie Zaidi began writing as an undergraduate, driven mainly by a desire to collect Participation Certificates at the annual on-the-spot poetry writing competition. The certificates would establish that she was an active student (as opposed to what?). The first year, she wrote a derivative poem in English, borrowing heavily from some Urdu couplets written by her grandfather. She was content to receive a participation certificate and to focus on group dances instead of writing. Next competition, she wrote an on-the-spot poem based on her own thoughts, feelings etc. To her surprise, she won the contest. She's written a whole lot ever since. Group dances were more fun though.

ANNIE ZAIDI

AT THE APPOINTED HOUR, THE BODY WILL NOT GO

like the arthritic woman relieved
she beat all her cousins in the end
the body goes on licking its lips
asking for leek soup and mashed potatoes

it asks to wear the shirt shot through
with green silk thread and pointy lace
and pink hello kitty underwear
a kindergartener on the first day of school

the body clings to the knees of the day
count down five four three two one
at the appointed hour the body blubbers
and begs for more just a little more

a black moon will wax at the appointed hour
and hands complaining of the slimy trail
left by destiny will burn with the fat of love
long after the body stops begging.

ANNIE ZAIDI

ESOPHAGUS

Your tongue gives so little away
What of the rising gorge?
Bitter years of gall?
Tell me how hard it was
to bite back what you swore
no man should swallow.

Give me pitted roofs
Give me a clue to the cavern
where your crouching dragons go.
Don't just say it goes too far back
for you to know.

ARJUN RAJENDRAN

From a hilltop in Stirling, Scotland, William Wallace looks through the hull of Arjun Rajendran's maritime poem; not far from the lake where the poet was attacked by a swan. As a child, Rajendran sabotaged his mother's submissions to foreign magazines by peeling away the stamps. His day job now entails training his dog to become a cosmonaut.

ARJUN RAJENDRAN

A BOY DISCOVERS ROYALTY

Alone after school,
I leafed through her
copy of Lady Diana's biography—
slick bikini photos came
loose in my hands.

All I remember then is
pulling out a bra from the washing machine
and trying it on. Placing my palms
over its empty cups, I imagined
I had the princess's bust.

ARUN SAGAR

The journey in this poem is an amalgam of many. The train is not a metaphor for life. Sometimes it seems that life is a metaphor for the train, and that the only true experience is one of dislocation, disjunction, migration. One is always in between, coming from, moving to. Sometimes it seems the only true experience is one of looking at the world through a glass window that frames and reframes land, field, station, town. Arun experiences a daily migration between his literary life and his 'real' life as a law professor. The window gathers dust, pigeon droppings. Sometimes it shatters for no apparent reason.

ARUN SAGAR

A SENSE OF LEAVING

Not a sense of leaving but a sense
of never having been
away in wakefulness,
the morning tense impressed
upon the present.
And in this lessening
of images–the
hills and fields unetched
with sunlight, there is no
you and I–uneven
walks in daylight or in rain–
the train itself a certain
sign of your fictitiousness.
And as in a test
of time involving trains,
two clocks, one
dispassionate
observer, I
move
not to arrive but to determine
distances,
            realities,
I am
watching from the tracks.
But we know the tracks
themselves to be in movement
to a larger music, a
'music of the spheres', you
might say, incorrectly, an
error compounded by
the train itself,

its oncoming.
And I am subsumed
in this fictional
departure
from a place in which I never
arrived, a chimera.
"Chimera", yes,
a fire-breathing monster, a
thing hoped for but illusory.
I have no way
to say it.

Cold breath in sunlight,
the sky flat and low.
Pop songs
on the radio.
Not a sense of leaving
but a coming to,
a myth-making.
I am confused by this
creating, remembering.

(A town, a hill, a face, faces.
Coffee on the street, mulled wine.)

The train has stopped
and I am awake, almost.
Plastic wrappers on the tracks,
a high-speed locomotive,
waiting.
I am confused
by this journey from the rational
to the lyrical,
                from the analytical
to you.

Not
a sense of leaving, but
a sense of not believing all
external indicia.
All findings to be assumed
false
until they greet you at the door.
Yes, the leaving is an act
of remembering, but
can we accept the converse
to be true?
Arun, I
dare you.
I seem to have slowed down instead
of speeding up,
already moving from the living
to the leaving,
and then to the reliving
and re-leaving.
Goodbye,
            blue sky,
autumn leaves.
(Families on the riverside,
afternoon drinking.)
There is so much to
tell you, but
what if the observer too
were fictional?
Not a sense of arriving, then,
but a starting in surprise -
there is no other
way to say it.
I am waiting
for a sense of unfastening,
unbuckling, unburdening.

Not a sense of leaving, but
a long, slow breath
never released.
(Long walks by the cathedral,
hot
waffles on the street.)
Not a sense of expectation, but
a sense of nearing
a pre-ordained destination,
a relieving from sleep.
(Long walks at
midnight,
hand in hand on the street.)
I need you to believe
with a sense not of
believing, but
a leaving your current location behind
at the speed of light.
Any faster and the train
will go backwards.
As in a watch that relies on motion, put
it down for a while
and listen.
I am looking directly at you
with a sense of trees unleaving,
the morning tense
receding.
There is a sense of cleaving
to the moment, I
have so many
ways to say it.
(Day-trips in sunlight,
wooden signs in the fields.)
Not a sense of leaving, but
a test

of eyesight.
Focus hard enough, look
hard enough
at where you were, to
get a sense of leaving
wherever you were going to.
I need you to believe
it's true.
I can almost see you
look anxiously around.
The train is already halfway
across the continent,
and you and I have lost
track
of how many stops remain.
Not a sense of losing time,
but a stepping outside
of it.
A sense of lying still,
then, a confirmation of
one's own existence.

(Hot chocolate in November,
beer glasses, thin stems.)

The train picks up again.
I am confused by this
coalescence of images,
not a sense of remembering, but
a momentary step
off the train.
Getting
right back on is all you
can do.
Think it through

to its logical conclusion.
(Green
hillside through a rainy window,
mid-morning tea.)

My stepping off has thrown
the train off course by an
infinitesimal distance.
(Black sweater, spectacles,
pearls.)
I need you to see it
as if with a sense of running
through the trees in twilight.
Each step takes you further
away,
the fading light a loosening
of your grip upon the present.
Not a sense of leaving, but
a turning around to face
the way you came, as
when the train docks in a final station,
a seaside town with no way out
but a change of engines,
a return.
Not a sense
of being in motion, then, but
one of tracing the contours
of the space occupied by your
receding self.
The experiment has been completed
and no conclusions may be drawn.
(The cathedral at dawn,

giant cranes above the station.)

It is a sense of leaving
a theatre after a show:
fully arriving is as
impossible as returning.
I need to believe that you,
too, are leaving
the present tense behind, that
it is a sense of grieving.
There is an infinite number
of smaller distances to cover
before I reach, each
an unbridgeable half
of what has already passed.
I need you to step

across.

We will not find each other, but
the effort may help us attain
the exact same
velocity as the train, close
your eyes and you will feel it.
It is a sense of leaving
a gallery where you
were alone and all was still.
I need you to embrace it.
I need you to walk beside
the track and watch
the train approach,
resisting the instinctive
step backwards,
looking
past me
towards my point of starting out.
I have a sense

not of leaving but
of leaning forwards into the track
after the train has passed at an
incredible speed.
A sense of staying,
then, in this almost-
destination.
An elevation of perspective–
a bridge, a roof, a hill–
to make the present visible.
I am an animal
that compensates for its
incompetence
with a keener sense of sight.
And now the day is etched
bright
with momentary sun,
a warmth against the skin.
I need you to come in
before the train hesitates
                    to a halt.
I need you to bring
with you a sense of
slowing down
to manageable speeds.
I want to climb
down with you ahead
of me, with
a sense of leaving
nothing behind.
Promise me you'll turn
around to see.
Promise me I will
return
and you will wait for me.

ASHWANI KUMAR

It was a dark and stormy December day in 1991. Augusta, George Gordon Byron's half-sister waited anxiously to meet Ashwani at the railway platform in the dead city of Deheri-on-Sone. Talcum-powdered, teen-aged Augusta wanted to tell her illiterate lanky friend that his fugitive verses carried a distinctive whiff of gunpowder. She knew he would not admit that he learnt writing skills from rats, reptiles, and insects. She kept waiting for him until the sputtering of the last coal-engine train disappeared in the evening. Years later, Augusta ran away with him and settled in a hill cottage. And Ashwani started writing regularly on his Grandfather's imaginary typewriter. These days, Augusta proofreads and edits his invisible partial- paralytic poems and quirky prose.

ASHWANI KUMAR

MUMBAI 2017: A LITERARY POEM

Distracted by unbiblical
unromantic, post-modern literary reviews,
we often travelled first person –singular
in the empty local trains.
Habit is a training you don't need
but still you practise it.
More so when soldiers in saffron robes come home.
Raise your hands if you have seen her.
One hand raised-What?
Stone in hand,
she is buried in the colonnades of ancient minarets in the sky.
In the darkness
I see her beautiful face behind the veil
distancing me from wicked memories
of the courtesan-queen of my village.
Ah, I was born in the cart of red ants
pulled by two dogs- the Present and the Past.
At fifteen
she pinned me to sleeveless Chinese paper napkins.
The first night was boring.
The Second night
I was hand-cuffed and executed by the nomadic firing squad.
In old age
all are happier than me.
They say I was always unhappy.
May be I chose not to dream
Not to hear any cries. I don't know.

In my prayers,
there are prophesies of strange verses raining in the desert.
A deliberate pause-

it is impossible.
I anticipate the news of my lynching.
Open the first envelop
the second envelop and the third envelop.
There is no letter-
only the timetable for a Monday.
Drowned in a pool of blood
I am a poet without a tongue.
Still, I try to lick my wounds.
I told you
habit is a training, literary or political?

BINU KARUNAKARAN

Binu Karunakaran was born in 1974 and grew up in Aluva, a small town by the banks of Periyar River in Kerala. He works as a journalist in Kochi and occasionally translates poetry in Malayalam to English. He was awarded the Charles Wallace Trust fellowship for creative writing in 2012 and credits his poetry to unrequited love: the scent of flowers of Indian Devil Tree, which grew in a compound next to his home and was sold off to a matchbox factory. He is yet to bring out a collection but imagines an anthology in which every poem is a matchstick. Black Swan is a poem about 'Being so caught up, so mastered by the brute blood of the air.'

BINU KARUNAKARAN

BLACK SWAN

Terraced night. Floating on the bean bag with your neck held
high, you resembled a swan gliding the dark waters of a lake. I
wanted
to hold you in a bone-breaking hug, but your wings looked
fragile;
in pain. A spirit not of this world with secret runes on its nape;
creature of mermyth—naiad, nereid, nymph — that shifts shape,
lies
in wait for the wandering monk-prince. Outside, the icy hands
of wind played notes of cello and lute: "Don't go, be there." My
brain swam with fuzzy Piscean fins in the amber that we drank,
the gold
we smoked. Desire came in waves warming the blood. Timid and
shy, I longed for your sleeping breasts, twin stray dogs with kind
eyes
and nipping fangs that turn eager when palms that feed opens
the door. I thought of kissing your razor-thin lips and feared they
would fade away like a healed wound; of rubbing my nose
against
the blackening, warm carbon smudge of your armpits; of
swinging from your belly's love handles—rails of a stair that led
to some secret recess in the blue of your heart; of tonguing the
balsamic folds between your thighs.

"Don't go, be there," sings the swan. The monk drops his robes,
steps into water. The ruthless prince draws his sword, guards the
shackles that hold him to earth.

DEBARSHI MITRA

Debarshi Mitra has since his childhood preferred the company of books to humans. His earliest and fondest memories are that of reading and time spent with books. Their physical presence has sustained him throughout the tumultuous years of adolescence. His earliest introduction to poetry was through the 'Romantics' and 'Tagore' as is customary for a Bengali household. Later in his life writing gave him the luxury of watching himself from a distance, a life lived retrospectively even in the midst of it, a detachment that has now become a central feature of his existence itself.

.

DEBARSHI MITRA

ENGLISH

I used to wear it on my head like a crown
when we went to my father's ancestral home
on some Sundays, the railways leaping in time
several centuries
taking us away from the city and to that other world
where concrete was sparse and the pale yellow of disease
left its unrelenting trace everywhere. Growing up in the city
there was little congruence I could find there.
Inside the house, surrounded by other relatives, sometimes
my (now dead) diabetic aunt would drag her body across
the hall to pick up a fruit kept on the table,
her eyes gleaming while she looked directly
at me and asked, " What do you call this
in English?"

DEBARSHI MITRA

CLIMAX

Once
the body
bent in surrender
its underside bare,
the animal
out of breath
gradually receding
wave after wave
along the shorelines
glimpsed all
in an instant.

DEVANSHI KHETARPAL

Devanshi Khetarpal was a high school freshman when she received the opportunity to study creative writing for a summer at the Corpus Christi College of the University of Oxford. Her teacher made her class read “A Dog’s Death” by John Updike. Devanshi, despite her fear of dogs at the time, started crying after reading the poem. Suddenly, she knew she wanted to be a poet. Poetry has, since then, taught her and led her to greater happiness, love, compassion and, recently, to greater healing. Devanshi now lives in New York and spends her free time roaming around the city, admiring and petting dogs on the way.

For more: devanshikhetarpal.co

DEVANSHI KHETARPAL

WHEN LOVING

I know you by
the sound of you

leaving

a river // longing
to be the soft, growing

forest //

dying, you place
your faith in everything.

DEVANSHI KHETARPAL

PRAYER

It will happen one day that I
meet you, as another one, as
a name, unheard of and with
meaning changed. You might
think I have been stolen. You
might go looking for me in the
darkest clefts, hoping I answer
your call. But each time, I shall
pass by the ring in your voice,
and pray I find you here. Again.

DEVASHISH MAKHIJA

Dead tigers. Dead hens. Dead fish. Dead cows. Dead birds. Dead flowers. Dead trees.

These are some of what keeps Devashish Makhija—and all of you—alive. Devashish Makhija is not dead yet. So he doesn't know if there is an afterlife. But if there is, he hopes the other creatures are in charge there. And not us humans. He hopes that they remember what we did to them back here. And he hopes that they are waiting to get even.

It should be fun. If you share his cynicism, he has many more morbid thoughts on justice for you (although not all of them are poetic).

For More: makhijafilm.com

DEVASHISH MAKHIJA

IF I KILL MYSELF TODAY

If I kill myself today

Tomorrow's milk will curdle
untended at the door

Some clothes in the
washing machine will stay
unwashed forever

A hundred ants will gather in
quiet celebration around some
spilt tea in the kitchen

A desperate doorbell
will fall from favour
on deaf ears

If I kill myself today

Dust will gather where my
broom won't be
reaching anymore

Ignored, a solitary banana
will rot, surrendering itself
to flies

A stubborn pigeon will wonder why
she's not being chased out the window,

and gleefully invite some
others in
Helplessly, three bottles
of pills will age past their expiry date,
their contents intact

If I kill myself today
A cellphone will beep a reminder
at 9 a.m. tomorrow
and every ten minutes thereafter
till its battery dies

A gmail account will gather unread
emails from known ids for years
before spam slowly takes over

A Facebook profile picture will find
that it never needs to be updated
ever again

But

The elections will be held on schedule

The monsoons will come again this year

My ageing father will grow even older

The building down the road will be redeveloped

Homes will be furnished

Furniture will be bought, will age, and be replaced

The unmarried will get married

The unborn will be birthed

Newspapers will be printed

And read

And recycled

Tomatoes will be grown

Soup will be made

The kind I was prescribed for a healthier, longer life

You will have it out of a bowl

If you have it next week you will shed a tear
in my memory
it will fall in the soup
you will collect it in a spoonful
and swallow it as you
choke, and break down

If you have it next year
it will be too hot
so you will blow on it till it cools
and then you will swallow it spoonful
by spoonful
as you sit before the television
watching your favourite dinner-time soap
cursing the ad breaks
with the same intensity as today
If I kill myself today
the telecast timings will not change.

DINESH SAIRAM

Investment Banking Risk Analysis' is not the usual choice of career for an aspiring poet, but Dinesh is both of them. In the spring of 2016, when Dinesh was pursuing his Master's in Finance, he met a girl in one of his classes, who was also a poet. They became good friends, often shared lecture notes and talked a lot. But the very best days were reserved for discussing poetry. Even today, Dinesh looks forward to that one stray text or call which is about cigarette smoke, stilettos or a thousand other things.

For more find him on Twitter @Dinesh_Sairam

DINESH SAIRAM

ICHTHYOLOGY

I smiled and shrugged
my shoulders, as if to
show indifference, when you
asked me if I would like
to go fishing with you.

I've never considered it
a hobby, not even a pass time.
I certainly appreciate the comfort;
the leisure of sliding the oars
back and forth, back and forth

over the undisturbed surface of
a stream or a lake, as you course
through the landscape. But how
is this made better by waiting
around peevishly for something

to swim by and be caught? How
is it anything but unsettling,
the sight of a silvery width
twitching from the gore of a hook,
its life now dependent on you?

For instance, imagine the first man who
accidentally caught a fish; imagine
his sleepless nights; the dying fish
staring into his eyes, the acute stench
of its rot forever in his hands.

HOSHANG MERCHANT

Once there was the Merchant of Venice and now there is the Merchant of Poetry. Hoshang Merchant, a student of Anais Nin nestles in Hyderabad, India. For anyone who had the opportunity to spend time with Hoshang would know that this fierce and feisty gay poet has his axe sharpened against loneliness. And of course, if you ever visit him, you won't return home without a stomach full of Biriyani and Azan from his nearby Mosque.

HOSHANG MERCHANT

THE LOTOPHAGI

The lotophagi
have heads between their legs
(So Homer said)
They go day and night
        looking for light
                between their legs
I first found them in India
                like Alexander
But they all belong to a single tribe
stretching from Bombay
                to the Bay of Naples
They're masked at Venice's Mardi Gras
And in the loos of Bombay's Victoria Terminus
                they hide their names
In Africa, they hid in the grass
                their heads in their ass
                        (like Ostriches)
But one look from your eyes
        Makes the light in their eyes flare up
        —Boy! Does it flare up Unforgettably
For even here
We're all one
        in seeking light
        Even the men who like ostriches come from eggs
        And go looking for light between their legs

HAMSI RADHAKRISHNAN

Hamsi Radhakrishnan grew up reading her father's poetry on Friday evenings after school. It was her favourite activity to do with her dad, and always left her feeling warm and comforted. She began writing soon after and learnt that writing about things gave her the kind of clarity she would have never found otherwise. Since then she has turned to poems whenever she felt lonely or confused, and obsessively wrote especially in the years she spent away from home. Some of her favourite poets include Andrea Gibson, Rudy Francisco, and Sabrina Benaim.

UNTITLED

I

We like to think so much.
Right now, we're made of all the things
we like to think we don't believe in.

You're the jagged end of a sword
dripping with the maybe blood
of all the demons in your head
that you would've slayed
if you weren't so afraid
of hurting their feelings.

We like to think so much.
And these days, we're only thinking ourselves into misery.
Drinking lies out of seeds
that would sprout into madness.
Hope is raw flesh that we've only been taught to
thrust our daggers into.

II

We were making homes out of humans,
every time somebody walked away, they left behind a door.

III

We were so busy trying to find
the ocean in the moonshine,
that we didn't notice we were entangled.
And when we finally wanted to unravel—
show the world we weren't folded at the center,
we had formed a knot from all our memories.
The further we pulled apart,
the more we were ripping at the seams.

IV

We like to think so much,
so we started thinking ourselves apart.
We felt our strings strain into slingshots,
our fingers stopped trying to find home.
How far can you extend your arms,
before they stop being your own?

V

We like to think so much,
we're now made of all the things
that we promised each other we wouldn't believe in.
Like vulnerability and forgiveness and everything
that makes the whole world feel out of balance.

We had never known how to fall apart,
so now we stack our stories on top of each other,
and ship it back home.
Today, I will open all the windows—
and when the wind blows
I know I'll hear it whisper,
even in our broken sisterhood,
we were twisted

JONA RAY

As a trained scientist turned to poet, Jonaki Ray has realized that both science and poetry have something in common—both integrate observing and researching until a conclusion, or some sort of (sometimes, a constructed sense of) truth, is obtained. She has learnt, therefore, to trust her instincts, and be governed by moments that move something deep within her, and to convert those moments into her writing.

In 2017, Jonaki was reading from her work based on events in her country to a room full of strangers in a country not her own. Yet, at the end of the reading, she realized that in the world of poetry a common thread of emotions connects everyone, no matter their origin or life journey. It is through this community that the realities of life make sense and offer Jonaki a chance of survival for which Jonaki is eternally grateful for the gift that poetry has been to her.

For more: jonakiray.com

JONA RAY

THE IMMIGRATION ROULETTE

The flags at Taksim Square gleam crimson
matching the fez topis on the staff of Hafiz Mustafa, 1864
packing Kunafas, Baklavas, and Locumas in painted boxes
Their eyes slide past the cross-legged women outside, waiting
for leftovers: food, money, and attention.
'Pay attention to the star-shaped patterns and water fountains'
say the guides. The lacy carvings, the jewel-like tiles, the
octagonal muqarnas,
the cobbled paths are jewels on the tours around the Alhambra
and Albayćin,
showcasing designs by Moors. Who were expelled by kings and
queens buried
in chapels built on what were once mosques.
The New Mosque on Galata Bridge—started by Queen Safiye—
an immigrant herself —
buzzes with tourists. The ferries have just come in. A couple
stops to take selfies. The wife clicks
her husband handing over his half-eaten ice-cream cone to one
of the kids trailing them.
'How lucky!' shout the other children.
Luck selects the twelve for a new life as the Refugees Welcome
sign blazes
white on Barcelona's Casa de la Ciutat ramparts. Turning away
from the TV screen
showing weeping, desperate men, women, and children, trying to
kiss the Pope's hand,
the man snarls, 'Who is going to give us a new life? So many
have crossed over to other
countries for jobs.'
A century ago, for the ship Komagata Maru

crossing over from Hong Kong, Shanghai, and finally, reaching
Vancouver, didn't work.
The passengers were thrown back, only to be greeted by bullets
in their own land.
A hundred years, apologies galore, and a memorial in a town
near Kolkata testify
that it's the turn of a magical roulette that decides:
Who is an immigrant? Who, a citizen?

JONA RAY

THE HOUSE WITH SIENNA WALLS

The sari is draped in the Parsi style
With delicate daisies embroidered on the *pallu*
that covers your right shoulder.
You sit with back straight and shoulders pulled back.
Your hair is coiffed into a perfect bob
perhaps done by yourself using the scissors and comb,
Made in England, still lying on the shelf.
Your gaze is direct—no flinching or fear in it.
Living alone, no husband or children,
styling hair of women—a first in the city—
You must have steeled yourself against
questions and glances, if not taunts,
multiplicatively more in those years.
It is fitting that your photo is placed in front
of a mirror—surrounded by sienna walls
and crystal globules floating from the ceiling
in the house that you left behind, as a place
for people to walk into and remember the conflicts in their life.
Remember, yet forgive, and learn finally, to love.

KIRITI SENGUPTA

Sengupta does not believe in a formal or informal biography, especially one that will accompany his poems in a journal. He was taken aback when he won the Rabindranath Tagore Literary Prize (2018) for a collection of poems, Healing Waters Floating Lamps, he had released in the year 2015. Pleasant or otherwise, he counts on the surprises life throws in, and loves to read poetry that does not match with his style of writing. Sengupta reaches out to the infinitude of continuance through his poetry and prose.

For more: kiritisengupta.com

KIRITI SENGUPTA

FROM BEING LATE IN CALCUTTA

As soon as you mark me
I'll talk about events
that guide me to the records
you maintain.

I'd say crowded buses invite passengers
from unscheduled halts.
I'd emphasize the number of speed-breakers on road,
and their poor performance in preventing accidents.

I'd tell you trains run late.
Signals are laggy between stations.
I won't forget to mention how
a sudden protest
makes the train stand still for hours.

I'd discuss about the day I reported late,
owing to instantaneous suspension
of underground train services
as a man killed himself on the railway lane.

I'd ask you to remember why I came late the other day.

If you can recall,
I had indigestion despite eating at home.
I blamed farmers for sprinkling pesticides on crops.
I pointed at my salary that failed to buy organic veggies.

And then,
I'd invariably argue about maintenance and population.

I'd appreciate China, one-child policy, and their claim on
how the government prevented four hundred million births.
And how India thrives on the revenues earned
from selling nicotine and condoms.

I'll explore other issues
the next time I reach late.

KIRITI SENGUPTA

TOURNESOLS

after Vincent van Gogh

Make them alive, I said,
give them the sun and a parrot,
if you think right.

At-least some gay yellow shine…
Wish he had listened to me

while he painted the sunflowers on canvas.

Life would not have stilled
had there been water in the vase.

MANJIRI INDURKAR

Manjiri Indurkar has been told her poems are even better than her recipe for Koshimbir, which she learned from an old woman who probably wasn't alive, but these things have never mattered to her. When she was on a writing residency in a small Finnish village earlier in 2018, all the felines she met there concurred. She once encountered a woman inside a book and fell in love with her. She now keeps her hidden, but if you are nice to her, she might tell you about this woman, who also happens to be her doppelganger, popularly known as Mary.

MANJIRI INDURKAR

DIABETES AT A BIRTHDAY PARTY

On a channel, a day late in celebrating
Lata Mangeshkar's birthday,
plays a song where Sadhana promises to haunt her lover
and Ma pierces a needle in her large stomach
pushing insulin into her body
diabetes, she reminds me, *will eat your bones.*

If you ever look at pictures
of those suffering from rheumatoid arthritis
you will find the bones parting ways from each other.
Ma's bones haven't begun that journey yet
but if diabetes wins this war of diseases
they may not have to.

This is not a good Lata song, Baba complains
so many songs to choose from and they play this
he complains the way Ma complains about the needle
that has broken inside her skin

Baba whose knees hurt when he bends them
is a perfect candidate for a Moov commercial
Aah se Aahatak
he says with a conviction
that has been practiced over years.

He claims to have reached the place
only Yudhistir could, but came back
because he isn't fond of dogs
because I was eating Maggi and waiting for him

His stomach is hard, dried-up in the sun
frozen in time
from selling daris to people.
He narrated an O' Henry story on his retirement

and everyone looked puzzled, but impressed
which Henry was this, they asked,
I, II, III, IV?
turning him into a historian when he
just wanted to be a storyteller

I was always cautious of not using Ma's comb
dandruff was contagious, I always thought
but it turned out to be hereditary.
Sometimes out of boredom
I scratch my head and watch dandruff snowflakes
fall on my keyboard.
my scalp bleeds silently as I pick the white chunks
spreading on my head like the map of Scandinavia

A different Lata song is being played now
Ma likes indulging in trivia
Priya Rajvansh was Naveen Nischal's best friend,
she informs her audience
Betaab dil ki tammana yahi hai
she sings complaining
about her broken voice that can't hold a note
diabetes, she reminds me, *will eat your vocal chords.*

And I wonder silently,
who talks about diabetes at someone's birthday party?
Ma's life is a cautionary tale.

MANJIRI INDURKAR

MY MOTHER SINGS DISCO DIWANE

When I am seven, Aai undergoes a surgery
to remove cysts blocking her breasts.
I fall asleep in the math class and dream of her.
She wears a hipster headband in my dream, like Rekha
in *Ek toh kam zindagani*, but sings a different song.
Rekha, my mother's namesake, tries to wake me up,
But Judy Jones, my class teacher, pushes her away
and I don't get a gold star for my homework that day.
When she comes back from the hospital
I ask her about the song she was singing in my dream.
She teaches me *Raat aur din diya jaale* that night,
and I win our colony's Sa Re Ga Ma Pa,
with popular consensus.
So I get to sit on the lap of Aazoba's friend
for as long as I like.
Aai's stomach bears three biblical crosses
from a recent gallbladder removal surgery.
With the stretch marks from two pregnancies
and several small scars from the insulin needle
crowding her stomach, Aai's body
is the bloodiest site of worship.
She complaints of being addicted to laxatives,
every night, she drinks 10ml of EMTY,
and jokes about it not emptying her stomach well enough.
She wakes up from her afternoon nap saying,
It would be great if I could pass some gas,
and starts singing *Disco Diwane*, as if
it's the cure for constipation.
Aai, the pop sensation of the 80s is back again today.
Ahaan!

MEDHA SINGH

Once upon a time in a smoggy fairytale, Medha saw a contrail of noiseless bats floating over India gate. This is was not so long ago, neither was it the beginning of anything significant. This is why she writes poems. Everything is a poem in the grip of her gaze, sitting in the ordinariness of things. A storyteller looks around, a philosopher looks to the heavens, a poet looks toward the earth. These claims don't have any scientific value, but they do have a poetic one. One day, she learnt the difference between the two, and subsequently looked up, around and down. There was a page where she finally let her gaze sit, to learn they're mere roles, each one played to make up for the clumsiness of the others. Nothing is learnt without solitude's pleasure dissolving in the mind. Don't ask her out for coffee, not yet anyway.

MEDHA SINGH

DEATH BY MANGO

My mother's doctor died.

He knew he was on his way out,
so he admitted himself to the hospital
where he spent his time saving or easing lives
consoling the old and infirm,

that a life well lived
makes illness matter little: go talk
to your neighbour, turn off the tv
stop lying to yourself, and it's all good.

Today, my mother ambles home
morose with the grip of grief
tightening around her neck
almost as though, she was meant to
save him, for he did his best
to do the same for her.
She has a sugar problem.

During a check up, long ago
he once told me
a grandmother was brought
dead upon arrival,
surrounded
by her grandchildren
all in tears.

Sweet thing, he said,
'God went easy on her rectum',
amid the deluge of Delhi summers,

she died, choking on a mango seed.

MEDHA SINGH

DEVIL WORSHIP AT A PARISIAN KIOSQUE

Every void is an opening;
always so gentle when it

starts.

Yet there you are

thick

in its nectarine viscosity: a spaciousness
now expands wider than your being's nest,

and your heart spirals tight
into itself, now begun to slide
into an emptiness, into soft light.

You enter this world,
wet and worried

still clutching at the fibers of existence
your hands soon relinquish an old home
suspended in an unfamiliar vacuum
the blissful silence of your mother's womb

Every one, of your skin's old aches
now gone, free of a familiar surface.
Your own white and pink tenement
retains your paralyzed, quivering flesh.
Eyelids shut, how the mind breathes
slow, as you float, in someone else's dream.

You open your eyes to get off the train,
hear the routine chatter of hissing, shuffling
feet as you return home burning, from work.
Crows encircle slow overhead, as though

you were dying, years withering
with every tomorrow.

Car noises, honks and vrooms irrigate
the shop windows where a garment waits
sans character, rests fully without you
in its empty sleeves, it calls you out:
your lover might not come home today.

He warned you of it the previous
night, and you'd let him walk his own way.

*

You light a cigarette as your eyes search
for a friendly kiosque. A man sits behind the counter

smothered among flapping stray tongues of newsprint
and quick, feisty winds. Old as the trees that scent the paper.

Shrouded in a fort of ink and magnets,
postcards and keychains—
he meets your glance,
as though he were yours, waiting
for you to bring him groceries,
anticipating being carried home.

You don't know him, he looks
as though he has half a life—

He could be your stillborn brother;
in him you see the pain of lovers trying

still to punish you with their silence,
over political differences and then some

with their insincere friendship.

In his assessing eyes, your dead father lurks,
their wrinkles drawn on by an ex-boyfriend

(who painted, sometimes painted you, to make
you quieter, he couldn't take your sparring;
and one day he tore up the canvas
when he began to hate you).

Wrinkles extend speechless, infinitely beyond
the range of a voix céleste from one Hausmannian window
lone, nearby, spelling constellations
that don't exist. The man at the kiosque

says many things without a glance,
so still, piquant in his pallid frame.

you find some remnant of a hateful minister
whose words you were very unhappy with.

You'd like, one day, to turn around, get off the bus
and walk your feet home—it would be nice

encountering a newsstand where the guy selling newspapers
is just a guy selling newspapers,
short of leaving your soul in tatters

You don't have to meet his gaze
when you light a cigarette,
and acknowledge the fear that
this might not be your life.

MEERA SAGAR

It was while she sat watching the sunlight play on the many-coloured windows of a church in France in 2001 that Meera's first poem came to her. Since then poetry has come and gone from her life, playing hide-and-seek, appearing and vanishing like a friend who calls every now and then. Both have learnt to be wary of their promises to keep in touch. Neither knows when they will meet again and meanwhile, life is the pause in an interrupted conversation.

MEERA SAGAR

ARRIVAL

You smell it before you glimpse its shape
outlined against the haze. The first breath
is dust storms in the gullet, but as you cough
and sputter, it gets easier.
                                        And then the clotted air
closes around you till you barely sense
the day turning to sap, how a fly persists
at your windscreen, the fading green
of bottles in a crate, or fruit skins swelling
                                        with something to say.

MOSARRAP H KHAN

Poetry for him was born when Mosarrap H Khan saw a chicken waiting to be slaughtered at a butcher's shop. Later on, he found poetry in the sinewy limbs of a man pedaling a bicycle and in the eyes of his lover. Since those uncertain days of youth, he has dabbled in poetry and enjoyed the process of unravelling his own fears, joys, and anxieties. Someday he hopes to find enough time to immerse himself completely in the art and craft of poetry.

For more: mosarraphossainkhan.com

MOSARRAP H KHAN

THERE HE SAT

He sits there hunched,
pretending to read a book written
in a language he learned late in life.

This is his way of reminding me
what keeps us apart – his now-found
faith and my indifference to it.

He smells of decay and old age,
like the house, keeping our secrets,
the white paint peeling off the ceiling.

The walls crumble here, the moisture
corrodes the bones, adding to
ruins of memories.

He will sit there hunched tomorrow
and the day after and read his book.
The wall will keep growing between us

MRINALINI HARCHANDRAI

Before being a writer, Mrinalini Harchandrai was a reader. And before being a reader she was a listener. It began at the dining table in her nani's Panjim house, where she was lovingly fed the journeys from conflict to resolution, from sinner to saint in her grandmother's narration of the parables of Guru Nanak. Back in Bombay, she looked forward to sessions in the school library where the librarian would read out stories to her class. Thereafter, she would escape the stone walls of school within the library, rapt in her own world, between the pages of this one and the one in a book. A habit fed further by her mother who got her a membership at the sole lending library in her neighbourhood; where she polished off books faster than she could borrow them. Now, she listens to the rhythms of the news and the streets; she reads the longings and journeys of friends and strangers. Now, writing, for her, is an incidental and happy byproduct of these early grooves.

For more find her on Twitter: @MrinHarchandrai

MRINALINI HARCHANDRAI

Excerpts from
CITY CYMATICS

II.
Together Apart

Frequency: Resonance occurs without physical contact.

There was leaking
through the glass sheet
between the skins
of our propriety
where I found
moments strung up
in tinny glints
where pressed bellies
ache and schlop
and bones lie
deep with magnets
and flesh folds
push on themselves
finding self-understanding
like echoes
ricocheting in trenches.

III.
Whalesong

Frequency: Sound below 20 Hz is infrasonic.

What characters
do you use
if you speak
in numbers?
How does 120
or is it 20
tell me how deep
the sound of you goes
all rattles and clicks
I find my way
studying the length
of your pitch
groping through
murky inks
since we live
in polar latitudes
of trust, decreasing
like Matryoshka dolls
to find mostly
codes, not Morse,
for solos.

NABINA DAS

Nabina Das thinks she is ginger root. Because rootedness is such a clichéd word for her. She spreads, connects, and travels in the cartography of her mind which vegetables cannot, being "rooted", and only a pungent, sharp, taste-altering ginger root can. Speaking of cartography, she imagines poetry to be her sole axis in a map-less world. Or, a pair of footwear she can wear as a flaneur to imagined territories. Probably poetry is her lover, one that no human can ever emulate. Because it lulls her, rocks her, caresses the senses, and creates more poetry for her, endlessly. In reality, Nabina finds it utterly boring to talk about poetry in a formal, straight-jacketed, normative set-up. Even as an instructor of creative writing delving mostly in poetry, Nabina lets poetry do its own talking. All poetry is political for her, hence she considers even the act of writing, ergo speaking out, a rebellion, an act millions are sadly denied around the world today.

NABINA DAS

APOLOGIES FOR OUR TIMES

Is there really time to say, sorry, we won't long any more or is there
more time for side-winking the Modis and Yogis as well as sleep?

We stalk love to get pained in return each time the heart throbs—
is there time then to say sorry to nature's well-designed tricks?

But I'm sorry for all the songs that I had composed, for imagining
children will live and the oxygenated world would be better one day

Where do I keep my apologies, if not on your lips, indeed—
for not loving enough, not saying enough that I do, yes I do

There may be times when I need to speak and still stop
look at the watch and imagine your jawline sharp in the dark

We must go our ways and at the station I watch the crowd, feel
sorry about the young men who lust me and just cannot reach out—

During my lone walks I notice wall handbills of the local quack
reminding me that I could still want a(nother) child of my womb

And the day goes by just as myth, all fire and rumble, TRPs
from news channels, and we're supposed to feel sorry anyway—

Apologies for swear words, screwed up plans, burnt toast
botched meetings, failed flirtations, and even the ISIS

Must we say sorry—soft, soft, say it soft—and retreat for love?
For you the Judgment Day, while I await his tender gaze.

NABINA DAS

MY NEIGHBOR IS A GAU RAKSHAK

Everyone has a gau rakshak neighbor these days
not everyone knows what they look like
we say happy Diwali sirji, and how's the weather today
we eat cake, madamji makes tea when we meet.
I could even have a lover who's gau rakshak so tender
that he keeps me from all untowardness of nights.
Our gau rakshak neighbor wears branded jeans
he hates Chinese goods but flaunts a Swiss watch
she too likes kitty parties where Ramdev churan churns
Zara scarves with Kolhapuri sandals for the ladies, kyunki
after all, Musalmanon me hunar toh hai for craft and art
thus my gau rakshak friends make light of life.
When we meet we say pleasantries like the rain
until my inshallah waterlogs their ears, they seem stunned:
You JNU-wallahs are like that only no, they say
a little wanton, a little awaara, somewhat misfit
still I recite Bhakti poetry and often placate the bhakts.
Our gau rakshak neighbor asserts Hindu khatre mein hai
the sky is saffron, cows can turn plastic bags to manna, and
The greatness of Bharat Mata in just one single meet
then Nirvana becomes a Bengali mithai he offers with tea.

PAULAMI SENGUPTA

On some days, an incoherent liquid trickles down Paulami's soul. She feels warm and wet and rushes to get hold of the nearest notebook. Words come out: like children, like ravines, like paper boats. Some in Bengali, some in English.

Paulami holds on to Delhi when Kalyani Simanta Local is about to reach Barrackpore. She talks about Dum Dum in Delhi metro and remains dazed with childhood terraces while in Bali. She just keeps trapping herself in memories and disentangling through verses.

Letters: paulami.sengupta@gmail.com

PAULAMI SENGUPTA

Excerpts from
PATEL NAGAR DIARIES

Patel Nagar at Night

Next time you enter around ten at night
You will see how Patel Nagar is buffering
for the morning next in neon-signed food joints.

Mannequins stand rapt in attention
As you get out of the cab
And ask for change in halting Hindi

Parks, parlours, and phone booths
Stare at you exhibiting nightly loneliness
That cannot be salvaged with samosas
As shops are closed.

PAULAMI SENGUPTA

Excerpts from
PATEL NAGAR DIARIES

Patel Nagar on Fridays

On Fridays
Patel Nagar is full of Patel Nagar
Noodles, condiments, biscuits
Sweaters, shirts, and trousers
Shoppers in their labyrinths
Feel happy and oily
Like puffed up bhaturas
In woks larger than life and weekdays
So that I can say
All the world is a Friday market
And I must buy my wares.

Knowing in Patel Nagar

I can smell my neighbour's soap
Houses are that close in Patel Nagar
Antiseptics and detergents
Intersect nonchalantly
As our bathrooms step onto each other

One day we might meet
Put faces to the non-white noise
Exchange borderline pleasantries
Without mentioning 'I know you use Pears'.

As of now let's not get bothered about
The sound of someone gargling or throwing up in another building
At 3 am.

PITAMBAR NAIK

Years ago a female in Kalahandi in Odisha, named Phanus Punji sold off one of her kids to satiate her hunger. Did her hunger stop? No. The nation forgot this. The number of Phanus Punjis certainly multiplied. In another heart-wrenching incident, a group of people was migrating to Raipur for a livelihood. They looked as if they were fleeing for life. The nemesis of hunger, pain, and exodus shocked Pitambar Naik enough to start writing 2013 onward.

PITAMBAR NAIK

PADDY FIELDS, PUMPKIN FLOWERS AND AN EXILED CHILDHOOD

Reminiscence of an obscure dark panacea, in fact that's confined
May be a chunk or façade of the dream still clinquants like an oasis
Her grandpa then grandma none she could see
She hardly recalls, where exactly from she learnt
Twinkle, twinkle little star…how I wonder what you are
Desire is the cause of sorrow, the Buddha said, why should she care about?
Does it matter to Asia, she desires, hankers and longs, and that's genuine
But surely somewhere there in between her childhood lies.

A patch of sky down, life thinly lollygagged, a weaver bird yet dares the storms
Her fate deserted her like the Buddha did to his wife
Puddles of ecstasy, long jump and high jump and kabbadi and the eucalyptus jungle
It's not a 4G era, her lonely friend a few dog-eared books, a tattered school bag
And a Panasonic transistor would bring the good tiding every day
Sometimes she'd go berserk and the broken kite would get puzzled
There in the armpit of the mango coppice.

Laughter and the joy of Lebanon, downward little murkiness, who cares!
Where can Asia retrace those post cards, inland letters? The flavours of her instinct

Govt. Odia Medium School and its substandard pedagogy
Those bald unproductive Paramanand and Biswanath masters were Asia's headache
Fiery buffalos gazed from the windows' of classrooms. She rushed to the past.

Boxes of toffees, patisseries and sachet of fun in the festivities were yet aloof
The trail of acridness here and there didn't change her to be a human
The smell of the pregnant paddy fields and pumpkin flowers electrified Asia
Her childhood, the past not extinct, got exiled there just as a blue lagoon.

PITAMBAR NAIK

COFFIN

Your backyard wears a lone painting of acrylic
A few pieces of medieval ghazals
The lilies ooze deluge of love morphine
Picasso's brushes, jam-packed with incarnadined hues
The Mediterranean Sea nauseates in pensive ambiguity
Since how long have you been quarantined?

Your make up box blooms the beauty of the seventh season
Rains take a few pegs of translucent tequila
That's a flimsy grotesque; you left that night with no treaty
Thenceforth the park, the street corners' coffee café
The nearest Malaysian massage parlour, all crawl with pain.

A surrogated river revives from a brief death
A little cathartic infatuation, heinously termite-bitten
A long life-size reverie through an absent hiatus
In the secret drawer where all those snippets
Those specially twisted laughter yawns
I am heaping all my sins there, that can be safely locked.

In your absence here I walk like a monk
In the lush pink bungalows, clubs, inns and bars
Sizzling peace talks with the my sweet enemies
Repentance the aftermath
You say peace a sick mind's attitude; a new season foliates
Yet, beauty plus vertiginous callousness
It's hypocritical here; yes even the spring isn't mild.
I tried to stop the time it carries my coffin now.

POORNIMA LAXMESHWAR

The first time Poornima was smitten with the idea of poetry was when she read the Vachanas in textbooks. Rich in meaning and spirituality, yet simple in diction, the feeling of surrender came naturally to this form. It was a door of literature that was accessible to everyone and anyone. She keeps going back to reading the Vachanas whenever she feels confused with what poetry must stand for.

POORNIMA LAXMESHWAR

WHAT IS IT?

Sleeping peacefully is a disagreement. Nightmares need a body to enter, nerves to hold onto, thoughts to decay, ferment and the darkness—stink whispers, whispers.

The murmuring translating screams of past is made of butterflies, birds and flowers. How the hell did the evolution end up with humans—scarring, deconstructing?

Fluctuating thoughts, fickle, disturbed over things that don't matter. Rape, violence, bloodshed, the ever so growing cacophony of whines—howling, fading, howling, fading.

Division of boundaries, division of roles, division of people, division of dreams. With every line that is drawn there are twos, fours, eights—bits, shards, pieces and more pieces.

Disconnected—you and I were opposites, parallels. My mind, a pendulum between the described sanity of the world and the insanity of my love

And it swings

Sense, nonsense

Sense, nonsense

POORNIMA LAXMESHWAR

SERIOUS RANT

What is it like to have conversations that lack the depth, the oblivion to meaning, strangeness of irrelevance, words failing into senseless sentences?

What is it like to act on something being indifferent to opinions, negating the piles of instructions, not minding the conventions, to surrender to one's own will?

What is it like to be unafraid of symptoms, venturing dreams, feeding on a triumph of war within, disowning the world around?

What is it like to be someone else, mismatching identity, dwelling insecurities, reverse thought process, disintegrating into nothingness?

What is it like to be love dissolved, dismantled emotions, uneven stories of origins, hormonal blames, unsettled harmonies?

I say 'eleutheromania'.

PREETI VANGANI

Preeti Vangani, since she was eight years old, has shared her father's obsession with learning up songs till their very last stanzas. But often, in the middle of their home karaoke sessions, she used to hear her father filling up entirely new sentences over the lyrics he'd forgotten. Years later, she understood that she too has the power to write her own words and give every 'old tune' she knew, a new meaning through poetry. After working in marketing for eight years, she has now anchored her life in writing and has performed her poems at laundromats, outside train stations, on buses, and in museums and libraries. She believes all public spaces need to have more poetry.

For more find her on Twitter: @Pscripturient

PREETI VANGANI

WATERLOGGING

I think about the mornings it saved me
to see children, splatter the Bombay monsoons
with paper boats, their miniature palms folding

into their mothers', two sizes too big, their raincoats
with dewy edges, hanging at the mercy of pastel plastic
clips. Zigzagging through a row of chipped roof huts,

the wiper of my second-hand purple car, outstretched
groaning its rubbery groan to drive away water from the road
ahead: cloud-gray, washed out, slipping into its own

bends; like a body being reborn when it lets itself break
down in full public view, each hawker and beggar negotiating
their wishes under the tick-tock of limited dry hours, flooding

this city, my heart, a closed island with eighteen million
impulses stirring, pumping in and out of crevices, to find refuge
under the radii of tin shelters or the hemline of an umbrella.

Inside, a water cooler sweating itself in the waiting
room, the slow drip of glucose reaching mother's veins, my hand
turning another blotted page, as Kundera says, love is the longing

for the half of ourselves we have lost. One abandoned shoe
floating in the slight rainbows of puddles. The doctor shaking
his pen as he talks about options. Does the sky know of all it lets
go

all it holds back and do my eyes? Walking through it all waist
deep,
students wading with backpacks over their heads, every lane
& by-lane, a canopy of escape routes. A 12-inch flat screen

TV being banged from the side. Intermittent cable service
and flashes of a news anchor lady asking the weatherman
for a statistic on the water harvested thus far.

PREETI VANGANI

SELF PORTRAIT AS FIRST LINES

My thighs are the train's general compartment. Everyone get on board
The uncle who holds my waist like nursing his whisky glass
[You are too attached to yourself]
A woman lives as a woman observing herself from the outside
From the outside it looked like we had a healthy sex life
The day he asked for a video of me pissing
I bought the smaller sized dress to look the part
How are you still so tight?
The jump to zip the fat under my jeans button
Intimacy really gets me off
And the man who gropes my side boob on the train
And the man who gropes my big bum on the bus
And the man who pretends to find his keys near his groin
And all the girls who wear the Women are Perfect T shirt
A knife under my pillow where milk teeth were hidden for wishes
To come true, I wish I hadn't shown him that part of me
Favorite Position: Low self esteem
A girl and her razor walk into a bar
Alcohol is a great equalizer
Vitamins, masturbation, and poetry
Love and marriage like clock hands, one chasing another
Brush twice a day
I care if I am kissed
A stand-up comic says to me: You have perfect porn star boobs
How do desire and repression mate?
Always in a trial room, I
A series of reflections, who won't talk to each other

REBECCA VEDAVATHY

The first book of contemporary poetry she read was a serendipitous hand-me-down from a friend's personal library on her twenty-second birthday titled A Working Girl Can't Win by Deborah Garrison. It was much later that she learnt that this copy was acquired from a bookstore in Hyderabad. How serendipitous to glean a copy of a book bought in what has over the last five years come to be her home, Hyderabad, from someone who lives in Bangalore, home to her for the first twenty years of life. She has come to believe that these cities and poetry have since then become an inextricable part of who she is, inspiring many of her poems through the serendipitous conjunction of these Muses.

REBECCA VEDAVATHY

AUTUMN BLOOD

Some days I stand in my choicest place:
a poem
with a leaf
I stand
and let the tree eat me.

Words hang like apples sewn to a tree –
the head of a poet – what was his name?
Didn't the goddess tell you, it's not safe to let
thoughts form words on your lips?
They aren't red like hers – betel leaves don't work.

Words draw shorelines on a passport –
the Syrian baby flattened on a sandy beach.
Didn't the griot tell you, children here
don't build sandcastles, anymore?
Lessons on geography and gore.

Words lay battered, dead against graffiti walls–
Dalit child and Muslim man.
Didn't the bishop tell you, baby cows are
called Mein calves now?
No, cow urine isn't red–enough said.

Words explode on the lazy newspaper–
shrapnel and body on boulevard–Paris.
Didn't the ambassadors tell you, you'll
pay for open borders?
They probably forgot–Gotham city in rot.

This poem has broken ribs and a lost ear.

Where shall I find it?
Beirut or Paris?
I don't want to stand here anymore.
The autumn leaves are mulched with blood.
Veins slit, roots flung. Run.
Left I scream.

The nation hears, pretends these are bad
words hiding in a pencil box–
learnt to be forgotten.

This poem has breath. It shall remember.
It shall eat the mud, the blood
democracy feeds us
and rise
into red autumn's green sister.

REBECCA VEDAVATHY

HOW TO PRESERVE CHILDHOOD

red monkey insides
part-time job: museum
fulltime job: friend

friend because monkey was not alive. he was a he though. i didn't name him. he was red. velvet. not like cupcakes. i am sure he didn't taste like cupcakes. that's because i tasted him. he tasted like fine red threads. touching tongue. tickling. he was as dirty as my feet. my feet went places those days. without chappals. climbed mountains of construction sand. dragged monkey's curly tail. a cursive 'g' with me. fed him sand. ate some. licked deworming syrup from measuring cups. bit around his black button eyes. an attempt to make them look like mine. he still didn't look like me. no one with three stitches for a nose looks like a little girl. that was the thing. he was a boy. i burrowed my fingers in his torn armpit. he didn't mind. like i said he was my friend. i told him my secret. pineapples are just big apples, i declared. that's why they have longer spellings. right? he heard me.

one day before convent school taught me "it is raining". "rain was coming". and when it came it came down with hail stones. no one was watching. i picked them up. one by one. silver sharp edges. taste of melting. white glass. tongue curled in cold. upside down camel hump. we didn't have a fridge. i marched to monkey. stuffed his armpit. he had an armpit full of hail stones. i forgot about. later when i looked for the hail stones. monkey was a soggy mess: a museum.

a year later, we bought a fridge. it came with a fridge box. bubble wrap. a cover. that year i played a fridge for fancy dress. the box was my body. i had lines and all. i licked ice from the freezer. it tasted like fridge. i never saw hail stones again.

monkey appreciated that.

ROCHELLE POTKAR

Dr. Fleming accidentally discovered that the fungus P. notatum prevented the growth of *staphylococci*. More importantly, it combated infectious diseases. This changed the course of medicine.

In just the same way Rochelle Potkar discovered poetry. It was first viewed as a contaminant to the petri dishes of short story and flash fiction. Only gazed under a microscope was it realized to have combated ennui, boredom, torment. Not only that, it was the sole proponent of enhancing qualia, filling existential sieves that nothing else could - not even air. It changed the course of Rochelle's life.

For more: rochellepotkar.com

ROCHELLE POTKAR

WILLOW WITCHING

In heat spell before ground swell,
trembling, a woman goes pillar to post
for horse-trots of drops that spell likes robbers.
Dust flying mildew against her veins, surging in damp linen,
like dermis of wet mongrels.

For the volley on asbestos.
"We'll find some place good."
Divination in gemstones and a witching rod.
Like the old rain man dowsing a hazel twig,
in the land of the babu's office.

She runs around the whole bureaucratic system
Like rain off slopes to cradle water
from flooded forests, water-boxing, pinning storms,
desalinizing brakish with layers of mud, at the very bottom.
Or importing by boat from rivers. (Ponds are goddesses.)

Rooftop proofing is her watershed moment,
plumbing, cisterns seizing water like wild tigers
for plants,
irrigation,
the laundry.

See the rain man too condenses fog, dew
while waiting for long-buried wells.

She now runs in the direction of a tsunami…
a river never reversing –
ridges to trap, crops to grow –
the parched becoming quenched.

She draws groundwater over glacial melts,
red-tapeism,
free of sediment.

Her hair open like a tidal wave. The rain on rhythm
in sodden paper boats, smiling at her reflection
in detention basins.

Rain against its own skin
– the world reopening,
skies re-beginning.

Oasis of home.

ROCHELLE POTKAR

KEY HOLES

We hide our wet lace behind a trellis of plants, our voices
honeyed from jaded soap operas.
Our requiems are parties inside our heads, earphone to
earphone.
Tolerance in the diorama of this rented place.
No door of solace or shame left open.

They will keep boyfriends. And.
They will come with trouble. And.
They will eat meat. And.

But sometimes we translate into vixens: late night-girls with eye
masks,
returning on the stairs–*shush*! the landlord is insomniac
to stilettoes and side slits of little black dresses,
books, menstrual cups, and spandex.

Who will take responsibility for them? And.

Emerald nights pass into agate mornings,
the sapphire of our head scarves and prayer mats
from insular to secular near our 2 by 2 boxes.
We curl each night against thoughts of saffron eyes, bloodshot.

If the nights fall over our skin, our bodies become bottles
of wine, with a crack against it. Dripping… dripping…

They will get raped. And.

Wooden cages with wooden birds flapping to horizons,
we scrape air like parchment,

peeling secrets from walls of adopted jailhouses.

They will grow wings. And.

Serpentine winds belching histories of women
who left when they heard the bricks squeaking,

Shush! And not again! And please behave yourselves.

But we play safe in dog-chewed chappals, our cycle tyres
gripping
the road's ruggedness
as alleyways sugar-lip the broken sky
of old whispering neighbors.

All this for only one proper peg to place the key
of our russet city-freedoms.

They will wear short skirts. And.

SARABJEET GARCHA

As a small boy, Sarabjeet Garcha used to consider himself lucky to have been born beside a river until he discovered that nearly all his schoolmates were equally fortunate, because wherever one lived in Nasik, the Godavari wasn't very far. Before he had turned ten, he and his bosom buddy gained notoriety in school for bursting into guffaws at moments that teachers found grave, if not outright soppy. Besides the frequent rebuke received for this weakness, Sarabjeet remembers his English teacher, Shirley Vaz, who made him fall in love with language, so much so that he read more Dostoevsky than digital electronics during his engineering college days. These days, he considers himself lucky for just being human.

SARABJEET GARCHA

THE INTROVERT'S EXCUSE

You get to be known
more by soft-spoken
waiters in a hill station
overnight

than by your neighbours
over years.

Intimacy comes
at a cost.
                But then,
what's a bargain

if you are not the one
                driving it?

SARABJEET GARCHA

CHARGED

Someday, I'll get to it—
            get to my oracular bit revolving
in the ionospheric orbit.

Up there, I'll unburden your soul
            of all earthly information,
buff up the silence

of cosmic bodies twinkling
            away into eternity, and
soothsay the evolution

of a world not governed by
            if-this-then-that. Save
your words till then. Climb

out of planetary plans to be
            embowered by desires
which have achieved

escape velocity.

SHIKHANDIN

Years before Shikhandin acquired the nom de plume, she was a girl—a girl who dreamed and scribbled in notebooks and diaries like any other. And, there was also, a boy in her life who took a walk one day with her, the first of many. Time flows. Relationships mature, evolve, and change. Sometimes they are reborn and renewed. Much like art and poetry threshed from real life and etched into fresh medium. Take this journey with Shikhandin, now. Hopefully, it will be one of many as she unspools her thoughts and feelings in words that seek to shift your—the reader's—heart.

THAT LONG WALK OF OURS

It began on a sunny, March afternoon,
with my English professor remarking
playfully that not a sun, but the full moon
had lit up the sky, when she saw me escape
the dreariness of a structured student life.
We probably took off in a bus to someplace
far away from them – the college, its mean
narrow hearted students and staff. Incompetent
teachers (except her), the snide asides
about my jeans by girls and boys alike
who secretly aspired to be as anglicised
as me while they spewed Marxist
platitudes. The digs flung at our taste
for English Rock instead of Rabindra Sangeet
and even Hindi film songs. Everything
suffocated us. Everything delighted us
in our insularity. They envied our freedom and
hated our nonchalance. With few escape
routes, we often dived into the movie halls
at the Esplanade. That day we watched
Al Pacino making love
to his Italian beauty. The strains of the love
song playing in the background stung

our skins until we shivered in our seats.
With bare pockets and purses, we walked
all the way from Dharmtolla to Cornwallis
street. You were glad to have a girl
who could match your stride. I didn't tell
you that I was walking slower than usual, and
what I really wanted to do was to jump, skip
and hop, which I finally did when I finally
caught the drift of your conversation. What
you had been taking such pains to explain. Surprised
that I had never guessed. Puzzled by this un-girlish
trait. And finally laughing, embarrassedly, you told me
to quit being a grass hopper. Or was it rana tegrina
that you said? Who does that when proposed to?
(Except that this was not marriage. We were
teenagers.) Is that what you thought then, turning
a rich maroon under the sun, as you
watched me? Or did it occur to you later
when you saw couples slow walking their way,
coy and ripe for sex at the same time, meandering
through the city? Years later, when marriage had
made a woman of me, and motherhood hadn't
managed to slow my pace, I looked back
to that ring-less, flowerless, candy-less afternoon.
The dust of construction debris. The garbage strewn
road. The not holding of hands. The matter-of-fact
admission, though long winded. And the parting

grin, as if we had together pulled off
a successful heist, and were sanguine that no one
would ever catch either us or the loot.
Our confidence that we would
carry on, picking up from where we left with
the same ease and assurance of bears
that have awakened from their winter sleep.
You never wore your wedding ring, because
your finger felt constricted. These days
my thickened fingers follow your example. Our
hands are free. We still don't lock them
together when we walk, except on one occasion
when I had a bandage on my knee and the stairs
were steep. We still match our strides, a bit
slower now, but as self-assured as before.
Our walking shoes worn thin.

SHRIRAM SIVARAMKRISHNAN

Shriram Sivaramakrishnan used to call himself a poet because what he wrote resembled poetry. But then he happened to read, among others, a certain Tomas Transtromer. He quit his IT job, and in 2016, completed MA in Poetry from Seamus Heaney Center for Poetry, UK. Now, back in India, back to his IT job, he is busy answering 'Why poetry?' with 'Nobody starts writing poetry, they end up writing it.' He now calls himself a poet because what he writes resembles nothing else but that.

For more find him on Twitter @shriiram.

SHRIRAM SIVARAMKRISHNAN

TO MONICA SELES

Hamburg, 1993

A nine inch knife
                                        is this long.
It went in   this far
between your shoulder blades—
0.59 inches of white space.
The reach of a preposition.

The remaining eight and a half inches,
you have to endure alone—
a bone-marrow worth of travel.
This distance

is not the same as you see here.
What you see here
is for representational purpose only.
In reality, it shall be your tenth Grand Slam

title—the unplottable one in your career Graf.
Though, you will not get a fairy-tale
finish of six-one six-love, straight sets.
Look across the net:

there is none to return your serve.
Your volleys will fall on empty valleys.
Your broken tennis racquet
is now a weed-land of wires no muzzle can graze.

And through this, you must trudge.
A game without sets. No six-loves.
Instead, you start with six million loves,
unsolicited.

SHRIRAM SIVARAMKRISHNAN

42,088

That's the exact number of bullets made
from melting the statue of King George III,
after it was pulled down by soldiers
during the American Revolution.

No records exist of the statue, except
for an inaccurate painting by a German artist,
Johannes Adam Simon Oertel. In it
the king sits in a warrior pose on horseback.

But this poem is not about the painting.

It is about the Forty Two Thousand and Eighty Eight
stories, waiting to be told, which is to say,
it is about one of them –

of ammunition made from a part
of the statue that had the King's crotch
in contact with the horse rearing beneath.

Such was the bullet's pomposity
that, at first, it failed to obey the gun
it was loaded with. Then the dynamics

of the revolver took over, and the rest
is rumour – that it had grazed a peasant
woman, and that later, she became pregnant.

SIVAKAMI VELLIANGIRI

When Sivakami Velliangiri was Sivakami Ramanathan she had enough bravado to present the then Mrs. D.I.G. with a poem about police torture in a flower bouquet. In her seventh standard she wrote her first poem on the 'kite' as she had forgotten the 'Kite' poem in her Radiant Reader; that year the School's Magazine was bound blue satin with an appliqued kite. Professor Srinivasa Iyengar included her in his History of Indian writing in English as early as 1980.

SIVAKAMI VELLIANGIRI

MY FIRST SMOCKED CHEMISE

In the cloister, the sisters
stitched their secret;
through pigeon-holes
we watched their thimbles
wondering if they were pears,
peacocks or push-carts.

Pastel shades of nylon
baby gowns with smocked busts
and baby frills alternated
with coloured embroidery.
Each stitch equally spaced
with computer precision.

The Sisters of Cluny
made a handiwork of art
handed over through generations
over-seeing the minute fabrication,
mannequins dressed up as Angels.
The ancient grey structures of Pondicherry
and the feast of all those Saints.
Most of all, the charity sale
my family indulged in clothes

from the nunnery of Christ-brides.
The white froth of the sea,
the washed out hue of bright colours
concocted to match a mingle of waves
rising like the dust of mud roads.
Padded necks patterned with curves
and angles, linings of soft linen,
and tiny loops for buttons
like the eyes of birds.

On the kitchen shelf
I see my childhood photo:

white frock and red rose
black frock and white rose
a toothless smile

and remember mother
who must have requested the photographer
to tarry a little, as she hurried
to the garden to picture-pick those flowers.

SIVAKAMI VELLIANGIRI

RAMESWARAM

Because you made us go to Kasi thrice,
because we made it full circle with Rameswaram
we were assured of a child. O stone serpent in the sack,
how we dragged you only to leave you under the temple
Banyan tree--two serpents rocking a baby Krishna to sleep.
I used to think it as serpents in copulation; you spoke
of the kundalini rising from the mooladhara, I understood it
as the Yin and Yang. We dunked ourselves is okay
but you dunked me in the twenty two theerthas, so that
I had to find a gap to breathe, you closed your nostrils
and dived into the sea thrice, I did not know how to hold
my breath, choked in the brine; years later
we went to Rameswaram to show off our children
also as thanksgiving; that stone-stupa that rests
under the great Banyan tree with hundreds
of other stone serpents, remains undocumented.

SNEHA SUBRAMANIAN KANTA

Sneha Subramanian Kanta has a predilection for impromptu poetry readings. While working on a video project for film-making students at Plymouth, a friend nudged her to read from a personal poem as an answer. Post-shoot, the pack-up metamorphosed into a diverse poetry reading. Along the same lines, a beautiful friendship was struck with a woman traveling to visit her daughter studying in China. Poem recitations were exchanged at Heathrow. Sneha appreciates the fluid space in which narratives of poetry may operate, and poetry carries through everywhere she goes. Sneha also most likely has a fitting quote for any occasion.

Letters: s.sneha01@yahoo.in

SNEHA SUBRAMANIAN KANTA

NITYA

for Kanta, my mother

I walked by the sea-shore, with reverberating sounds
from Eliot's Wasteland and its usage of Sanskrit words

and remembered my mother and I going to learn the
language.

It was evening even then—inscribed in an elegiac meter;
the soul was eternal, time; ever-changing and temporal.

The teacher, a long white-bearded fellow, an off-spring of
the samsara, turned away by its own cocoon often paid emphasis

on syllables that must be stressed—like some natural
emergency beckoned attention. My mother, a connoisseur of

languages and linguistics, carefully took notes. How we walked
the lane to our abode in the government quarters, her hrit
pundarika

beating fast to the pace of incomplete chores—my stotram for
her,
unknown to her, still incomplete.

SNEHA SUBRAMANIAN KANTA

HOW MY FATHER PRAYS

See, how moths eat dark
devour dusk contours
like raised fragments from a cashmere shawl.
Call me Ishmael, I tell my father
speak to me in a mouth full of Persian dialects
mumble

but my father is a silent man of great faith
in God. He tells me the ship is at a certain distance from land
because God wills it so.
Upon the knee of a ghazal
in pastiche stitched emulsifications of synapse ships
the sea is vacant like land
there is no grimoire, nor the steady onslaught
of rain.

My father supervises the symmetry
of a small-lodging night room in the ship,
I ask him of the openness of space and the shape
of stars. He cusps his hand in prayer and points etherward.
Dawn disseminates in soft pores
over ancillaries of his phalange as the warm sun
rises eastward.

The ceiling of the ship lathers with froth formed dayclouds
my father withdraws to a quiet spot
with psalms from a Dravidian text
invokes God from the mosaic of skies,
and then breaks bread.

SONNET MONDAL

In July 2014, when Sonnet got married and divorced after a six-year long relationship, the unpredictability of life came down harshly on him. A person who kept on searching for rat-holes to hide and escape from the crude realities of life finally stepped out of the country and met a Brazilian poet and filmmaker Marcio Andre and an English poet Harry Man, who inspired him to steal a boat at midnight at Lake Ohrid in Macedonia. He is still rowing in that boat across borders, absorbed in the profoundness of experiences while enjoying the inconclusive with his partner—poetry.

For more: sonnetmondal.com

SONNET MONDAL

NOBODY SPEAKS OF YOU SYRIA

You have shrunk to a handful of wet dust—
wet from tears and rapacious semen.

The heralds look at you as a whore

and your screams have no walls
to enclose their echoes. All have fallen.

Your ovaries are dead.
Your ribs have turned into razors
wiping out your sentiments.

The bullets you have consumed
have rusted inside your womb
and stained the colour of your blood.

Civilization looks as blank as
a dry river
that doesn't thirst for rains.

Somewhere in your ruins,
hope peeps like a thief
through a broken tooth
of a child, smiling at a broken tank.

Through her eyes—

You look so lean Syria,
but your history is getting fat.

SONNET MONDAL

THE HOMELESS

Split bolster, tattered shoes
a lean bed sheet —

the ménage of the homeless
sleep together.

He keeps mumbling
to them and asserts

I don't seek charity —

esteem, power
not even coins or food

but someone to chat with

for my ossified abilities
to grip sunshine

SOURADEEP ROY

Souradeep, of late, has been thinking that poetry must exist outside of the poet's life. He has arrived at this conclusion without really reading Roland Barthes well. He is, however, also sure that he writes poetry to explore *an* inferiority (you can also call it an inner life) through language and often falls back on the lyric for this reason. He certainly enjoys translating poetry more than writing original work. He is an academic and, like most academics, has a boring life with hardly any interesting anecdotes to offer. Except for this: he began writing poetry by writing love poems, and, on showing them to the woman they were for, was told, I love you very much but these are not good poems. He does, however, believe in love but hasn't read Barthes or Alain Badiou too well for that matter. He also conveniently those poems "juvenilia" and tucked them away.

For more find him on Twitter @souradeeproy19.

SOURADEEP ROY

A HISTORY OF MIRRORS

The first mirror was shared,
inside the hostel—it had white
lips frothing with Colgate staring back.
The second was rented and broken;
his reflected face too broke in the one
half that remained of the mirror.
The third was grand
and expensive, and rented
of course. It was this that
provided the luxury of
reflecting his entire torso, down
to the growth of pubic hair
below. He stared into this
one for prolonged minutes and,
on the day he turned twenty three,

witnessed one strand turning grey.

SOURADEEP ROY

REMEMBER/ IN MEMORY OF

Remember the arrival of spring:
the ceiling fan suddenly resuscitating
opening its eyes, breathing,
coming back from a coma.
The ceiling is no longer a still life,
the ceiling is alive.

Remember what spring was last year
the arrival of sunshine,
the end of winter chill,
the end of a course of medicines.

Remember the struggle of sleeping without Trika,
the onset of dreams. Remember, remember,
what a change it was
to have the knowledge of sunshine
on your skin.

This spring, I am fine, shocked at the ease
of being sane.
My depression left as it came: without a warning.

It left when winter left the city.

SRILATA KRISHNAN

Though Srilata has been writing practically since the time she was able to hold a pencil, she is still not quite sure she is a writer. She lives in perpetual dread of being caught out. If she writes poetry at all, it is despite herself. Srilata also teaches in an institute of Engineering which, perhaps, explains the perpetual dread. When not teaching or composing accidental poems, she is busy failing at her job as a mother of two. The family has given up.

Letters: srilata.k@gmail.com

SRILATA KRISHNAN

SIAMESE TWIN

Do you remember the day it rained
like it would never stop,
and you and I on Mango hill
watching her cling to her still-born,
and me wondering in my swimming head,
Which one of them is dead dead?
and both of us thinking Siamese twins
with our common seeing-dreaming eyes,
and you saying, too quickly,
"Such love is common in the monkey world."

Such love. Such love.
The phrase like a loaded gun,
and both our hands on the trigger.

SRILATA KRISHNAN

BEING SEVENTEEN, BEING BOYS

It's cricket in the blazing heat
and they are back,
a glisten of faces,
grime-trail on the bathroom floor.
Over tall mountains of rice,
a brief hungry silence,
and then, the ribbing-each-other
about school crushes and missed catches.

And to think that they are done,
nearly done,
being boys.

SRISHTI DUTTA CHOWDHURY

Genres and narrative devices are currently gagging her content. Srishti is either too greedy or simply too in love with non-sequiturs. She writes to navigate, eats to become & translates to move through the fabric of languages. Against the glen before Three Sisters, she encountered strange ways to peace. One child, waiting on her father before the church, gathered nameless flowers gently to her and lulled heathers to sleep. Religion and nature, the two oldest repositories of meaning in human life, is borne by the medium of language. Poetry is her shrine, her method to peace.

SRISHTI DUTTA CHOWDHURY

HOW TO LOSE A CAT

no longer perturbing how mother
can spew truths, twenty a minute, like
how i failed to fetch her finger from the station,
how i must accommodate dinner conversations with
the father, like how unspooling her threads lead to bad blood
about
old cousins, the dead brother, one aunt molly and that night
i wanted to be a hero. we all know how that ended, in canned
soup and
exacting the first broken tooth. a sink of bad blood.
no longer doubt my mother combs truth out
like obstinate lice, alternating care and force like gran's
mixer-grinder. like her varicose beseeching me to let
open the river, like it is normal. or what it is.
having a detective for a mother is work. not for her
service pistol that killed the cat. much less for her complaints,
like how
how she left me a heap of white, piss stain on a cushion,
one scar. i could be the hero but
it was my hand it was one shot
the father looms large

SRISHTI DUTTA CHOWDHURY

AND ELSEWHERE

july never ends, my lines

how disturbing the thought of climbing trees to pick one

bad apple

and slowly stripping to the wind.

how lifting up the skirt, the crime scene evokes the picture of
calm. fence by the sea, wooden

chair by the door, a book half-open by a thigh. this is suicide. the
need of which is met in this word and how.

how to slake my disembodied appetite, how to draw the line. my
writing is flawless surface. cut in to find nothing. bones.

so much transience cannot find its semblance in record, i let it
sail.

florid nothings

SUDEEP SEN

Sudeep Sen's late father was a historian, and a keen gardener and rosarian—his mother, a philosopher. They and his grandparents were all keen on reading poetry aloud from memory. Needlessly to say, Sudeep grew up in a typically Bengali home full of books, music, art—alive with discussion, recitation, food. As a very young child, when one of his favourite rose plants was disfigured by a passers-by—he was so affected that it made him write an elegy, his first poem, 'The Rose'—thus starting his 40-year tryst with the world of poetics—its music, texture, cadence, form, passion and magic. He says that he did not choose poetry, but poetry chose him—it's his mental health condition, his life-blood.

For more: sudeepsen.org

SUDEEP SEN

DISEMBODIED

1.

My body carved from abandoned bricks of a ruined temple,
from minaret-shards of an old mosque,
from slate-remnants of a medieval church apse,
from soil tilled by my ancestors.

My bones don't fit together correctly as they should—
the searing ultra-violet light from Aurora Borealis
patches and etch-corrects my orientation—
magnetic pulses prove potent.

My flesh sculpted from fruits of the tropics,
blood from coconut water,
skin coloured by brown bark of Indian teak.

My lungs fueled by Delhi's insidious toxic air
echo asthmatic sounds, a new vinyl dub-remix.
Our universe—where radiation germinates from human follies,
where contamination persists from mistrust,
where pleasures of sex are merely a sport—
where everything is ambition,
everything is desire, everything is nothing.
Nothing and everything.

2.

White light everywhere,
but no one can recognize its hue,
no one knows that there is colour in it— all possible colours.

Body worshipped, not for its blessing,
but its contour—
artificial shape shaped by Nautilus.
Skin moistened by L'Oréal
and not by season's first rains—
skeleton's strength not shaped by earthquakes
or slow-moulded by fearless forest-fires.

Ice-caps are rapidly melting—too fast to arrest glacial slide.
In the near future—there will be no water left
or too much water that is undrinkable,
excess water that will drown us all.
Disembodied floats, afloat like Noah's Ark—

no gps, no pole-star navigation, no fossil fuel to burn away—
just maps with empty grids and names of places that might exist.

Already, there is too much traffic on the road—
unpeopled hollow metal-shells without brakes,
swerve about directionless— looking for an elusive compass.

SRIVIDYA SIVAKUMAR

At age seven, with her poem, "My uncle is thin and looks like a pin," Srividya Sivakumar believed that she was destined for a life in rhyme, in whatever shape or form. But soon she realized that as a poet she should embrace every aspect of writing—the frank, the profane, the sensual, the carnal, the needy. As a result, her poetry has become a home to exuberance and annoyances, love and lassitude, want and wistfulness.

Letters: bookofpoetry@gmail.com

SRIVIDYA SIVAKUMAR

PAMUK PLAYS THE PALANGUZHI

I talk to him about Vijay Nambisan. Reclusive poet. Older brother.
He says there are many like him in his state.
Ayyappan died on the streets. Chullikkadu was a warrior. And MT is the greatest of them all.
"You English literature convent educated girls–step outside and look at the world."
My 'convent' was a government school with a ghost in the bathroom.
The marble floors were broken cement and cobwebs made for great hair ornaments.
It was first come first serve and the days you were delayed, you squinted at the board in a dimly lit space, wondering about arithmetic.
No one taught me poetry then. It was Mr Bell and Mrs Bell. It was Kutchu and his glasses.
English literature was a father's well-annotated Shakespeare. It was *Murder in the Cathedral and Gitanjali.* It was the state prayer, the few words of Tamil I could only hum to.
I know not of Bharati, the man I share a birthday with. I know not of Sangam poetry. I immerse myself in the wine of *Madhushala* and look for the *saki.* I sense the birth pangs in *Tamas* and read read read.
Yes, I'm not partial to your tongue.
But I can quote Umberto and Wislawa, Neruda and Saadat.
Life doesn't come in one dialect. Neither does love.

Neither does learning.

Neither does hubris.

Poets live and poets die, penniless in any language.

SRIVIDYA SIVAKUMAR

IMPRESSIONIST

A Jackson Pollock painting walks into the diner. It's jarring in its chaos and comforting
in its method. Senses slowly drip into sharp focus like an overloaded coffee maker with
cheap green beans and no palm civet in sight.

The eggs are surrealistic and beg the adornment of art and artefact. The plate is chipped
and dipped in olive oil from sustainable farms in the east.

It's all an act of persuasion to belie fears and soothe jittery nerves shot up with too
much strong coffee and no sugar.

Give me a kiss, he tells her.

She removes her eyeteeth and her lips are unicorn breath.

Let's touch so my colours bleed into you and your spices mix into me.

A painting walks out. A Modigliani nude, it hangs askew in a brown study.

SUHIT KELKAR

Like most poets, Suhit Kelkar lives two lives. In the daytime, he works for a company; in the evenings, or whenever he can, he writes. It may be that his salaried work produces no beauty; for certain, his poetry makes no profit. That these opposite selves dwell in the same skin is a marvel. They take a pause from seeking to obliterate each other, and realize that it may be neither could exist without the other. But is this a false belief?

SUHIT KELKAR

SHRINE

At the end of the street
there is a marble shrine

with no gods within.

Sitting silently beside,
only a cement mixer

baying at the moon
Soundlessly

SUKRITA PAUL KUMAR

Eight days on a sea journey. From Mombasa to Bombay. With no land in sight, in the middle of the deep blue-green ocean, Sukrita's adolescent eyes followed the little flights of luminous fish as they hopped from one end to the other continuously for hours on end. Standing against the railing of the deck alongside the ship, Sukrita watched musing: Where were they heading? Was there a destination? Were these mere playful swings? These were the take-off moments for Sukrita—meditations that brought forth her poetry. Even today, when she sits down to write, those reflections guide her way.

SUKRITA PAUL KUMAR

ALEPPO, SYRIA

Inside Al-Madina Souq
The market that once glittered
With silver coins and golden gifts,
Chocolates and popcorn
Lingerie and skirts
lay toppled from
somersaulting shopping trolleys
caught between
cannons and rocket warfare

Mounds of dried tears
stuck in hollowed eyes
gape into the stony void
of the tomb
Rosy cheeks by the hundred,
Split by bombs and explosives,
Wrapped in dust and scum
Plead for the kiss of the lover,
the lap of the mother

In the web of cracks
On the walls of the
Citadel of Aleppo, the piercing
Screams of children vibrate
Into the alleys, like lightning
up and down
And sideways, with no relief
In sight

Simply Urbicide
said someone…

And the Great Mosque
Is chock-a-block with the paralysed prayers
Of rebels
and soldiers

The rest are crowds of
left-over
women, men and children
fleeing with their prayers
rolled up in their sleeves
babies and bags on their backs

they float
and don't come ashore
they walk, they run
and don't arrive
they alight a plane
and don't land
they are embalmed
and remain entombed

they are refugees
forever afloat
outside their homes
far away from Aleppo
where their passports and
identity cards burn in bonfires

SUMANA ROY

Asked by her six-year-old nephew about the meaning of poetry— which he thought was a kind of tree, like the mango—Sumana fumbled for an answer. She showed him a poem (it's easier to show someone a cake than explain what it is, after all), but he wasn't satisfied. Why were they wasting paper? he asked, pointing to the space left after lines. Fumbling for a response once again, she said that that was how lines were cut in a poem. How do you kill the line —with a gun or sword? he asked again. She didn't know—she had neither of these weapons. You can press on 'Enter' to 'cut' it, she said, an epiphany having suddenly come to her rescue. Will they be cut if you press on 'Exit', too? the little boy asked, having entered the world of antonyms in school recently. Sumana thinks hard before 'cutting her lines' now.

SUMANA ROY

I WANT TO BE A TREE

I want to be a tree.

I know that this desire lives outside the curriculum.
Irrationality is man's favourite home—
One man's love is another's superstition.
I am the tree that wears passion's baggy clothes.
My hair soaks fear, my leaves the planet's poison air.
There is memory, always half-eaten,
and there's sleep, inevitably rural.
There's also sunlight, always a neighbour.
It's summer. And so the road's deathless fever.

I want to be a tree,
as naturally branched as the body's posture in sleep.
To woo birds—they avoid men and motion to sit on trees.

I'm leaning against a statue of sunlight.
The wind affects us unequally.
I wonder why tree branches
do not behave like curtains in the wind.
Or why we fail to hear creepers knocking at the door.

I want to be a tree.
The wind escaped being written.
The fire's autograph, the shriveled sunlight on trees.
Seasons arrive like prompters in a play.
The trees perform without the need to pluck claps.
I am an extra filling out the frame.
Change, cycles, the spiky heads of moss,
the menstrual stillness and the piracy of affection.

I want to be a tree.
Air a doll between my leaves,
prayer as inconsequential as mimicry.
Only blood needs religion.
And so there is none among plants.
Only love, as accommodative as a paragraph.

Love needn't be reciprocal—
How else can we love the dead?
The earth loses ownership of dead trees.
I imagine my funeral sometimes.
You, for whom the guitar is an integer of sadness,
you who thought I was invincible like crushed paper, saying,
"My world has lost its chlorophyll".

SUMANA ROY

TREE SAP

You can tell the age of a person from how he spits.
You can see how infants are beginners—
how their drool is everywhere, how it makes mush of contexts.
And so with tree sap.
The awkward sprouting from everywhere when sapling—
stem, leaf, bud and root—
unlike an aged tree's leaks: proper, sombre, tidy,
like blowing your sap into a hankie.

With age everything turns viscous.
For hardening is a marker of age.
Knuckles, calluses, sores, scars; and the heart.
Madness is loose, fluid, it easily finds itself a home.
But not wisdom—maturity pickles, needs a container.
And so the viscosity of tree sap, the density of ageing madness.

When tree sap flows, your ignorance about the foreign grows
nests.
For you are never sure whether it's a signal for beginning or end.
Sap is the tree's puppet, like tears are to the human heart.
Sap, noun and verb, and the difference in between.
Sap is loan and debt. (A half song is also a song.
For when you are angry, you are still yourself.)

Once, the light became beautiful by resting on you.
Now it's solidified into sap, turned white.
And you've become canned food, a future without bones.

URVASHI BAHUGUNA

In 2010, the poet Nitoo Das held a poetry workshop at the university Urvashi was attending at the time. The reading material comprised of several contemporary Indian women poets she had never encountered before. This introduction to the deeply personal and hyper-local work of Sharanya Manivannan, Sridala Swami, Meena Kandasamy, and Anindita Sengupta amongst many others challenged and changed her understanding of what a poem could hold. Around the same time, she became close to another poet who wrote of windows, earthquakes, and cats, and her friendship with Sohini Basak kept her close to writing even when her life concentrated on other matters. In the following years, she turned her attention in her poems to her memories of growing up in Goa, to familial complexity, to the ever-changing terrain of relationships, and to environmental change. Her poems are a result of those early meetings with writers and writing that resonated with her.

URVASHI BAHUGUNA

TERRARIUM

What we knew for certain is that Mr. Joseph pushed us
as hard as the boys. He expected us to slice the sky

as cleanly to slip our bodies into mud as willingly
to taste the dessert of a win as raucously. Our screams

filled the football field with pride. I don't know how
many of us still empty our lungs. But we know the feeling

know where to find the spigot. Other girls were good
at reading litmus paper or reciting the Constitution

but we had the world at the instep of our sole. We knew
how to curve air around the planet knew how to send

moons to halo the earth. In torrential rain not even the
sharp teeth of our shoes could keep us from slipping

into brown slush. Mr Joseph commanded we wipe
the mud from our eyes keep playing keep swinging.

VINITA AGRAWAL

In 1987, Vinita first exchanged letters with Jayanta Mahapatra, the eminent poet she had admired from afar. She was in college then, embroiled in political science and economics. But vines of poetry were blooming in some unnamed corner of her heart. She'd always written poems, but her verses were closeted in velvet diaries. Reading the finely crafted work of Mahapatra made her believe that writing poetry could be taken to another level altogether. A few years later, her poem was accepted for publication for the first time in Femina when Kamala Das was editing its poetry page.

For more find her on Twitter @vinita65

VINITA AGRAWAL

ARTIFICE

We shed paper shredded scars against the weather
Against ice
Flaunt our delicate remains
draped in crepe.

A fetish lattice
of sheer, sheathed sucked-sin skin veins
a prick-seam of open sores
a stripped self, all go on display.

Whipping off eggshell veils
lisping a disjunct entity
inward sprinkles of sticky confidence
priggish in a carnival world of lust, we are lost.

Pillage, spillage on earth's pudge
Still rainbow words d r i b b l e daintily
from sky's open snout
as crystal lips commence sweet talking.

CINNAMON & SYRIA

The farmers first shave the outer bark off the trees
The enemies first kill the men of the country

and then shave off the inner bark
and then wipe out the women and children in a bloody narrative

When Cinnamon is dried, it naturally curls up into "quills."
When a child dies, it naturally curls up into a Cassia of horror

Those quills are then cut into sticks or crushed into a spice powder.
The prewar population is then displaced, brutally tortured

The cinnamon is dried for use
Damascus is dried to ashes…Euphrates dried to a stony bed

People incorrectly conclude that Ceylon cinnamon is real cinnamon
People incorrectly conclude that real Sarin (C4H10FO2P) won't be used in Syria

It's not. All cinnamon is real cinnamon
It is. All chemical weapons are Redlines now slashing the holy Tigris

80-90 percent of cinnamon comes from Indonesia
80-90 percent of ruins are in Aleppo

Cinnamon can be used as a room freshener and a moth repellant
Cruise Missiles can be used as gut slicers and Mosul marauders

Cinnamon can be used both as a spice and a medicine
War can be used both as an end of humanitarianism and a
beginning of hatred

Whatever you do with cinnamon, just please don't try the
cinnamon challenge
Whatever happens in war, just please don't think that people
have a choice

Cinnamon, beloved spice
Syria, beloved land.

ACKNOWLEDGEMENTS

Poems in Best Indian Poetry (BIP) 2018 have been published with written permission from respective authors with previous publication credit duly acknowledged. We congratulate the editor-in-chiefs and poetry editors of the following journals & literary magazines. We look forward to many more new voices in the years to come.

Below are the names of journals and literary magazines that appear in no particular order.

The Bombay Literary Magazine, Setu Magazine, Cha: An Asian Literary Journal, Vayavya, Bangalore Review, Dissident Voice, Hakara, Antiserious, Muse India, Noble Gas Quarterly, Scarlet Leaf Review, Ainanagar, Plume, The Aerogram, MadSwirl, Coldnoon, Kashmir Lit, Tree House Arts, Francis House, Anti-Heroin Chic, Mascara Literary Review, The Daily Star, Right Hand Pointing, Bird's Thumb, L'Éphémère Review, Figroot Press, Poetry at Sangam, The Galway Review, London Magazine, Elsewhere Lit, Guftugu, Little Troller Books, The Bombay Review, WordPeace

NOTES

NOTES

Other winning titles published by
RLFPA EDITIONS-

RL Poetry Award 2017

Teaching Father how to Impregnate Women *by* Soonest Nathaniel (Nigeria)
Mother Tongue: Apologize *by* Preeti Vangani (India)
Editor's Choice: Betel Nut City *by* Shalim Hussain (India)

RL Poetry Award 2016

Somewhere but not here *by* Stephen Byrne (Ireland)
Apostrophe *by* Barnali Ray Shukla (India)
Editor's Choice: The Land below Water *by* Manik Sharma (India)

www.ingramcontent.com/pod-product-compliance
Lightning Source LLC
Chambersburg PA
CBHW050016170726
48282CB00025B/427
* 9 7 8 8 1 9 3 9 2 9 5 0 6 *